PRAISE FOR *BE THE BEST PART OF THEIR DAY*

Dr. Schreiner's *Be the Best Part of T[...]* case for the role of positivity, appre[...] leadership. He offers practical strategies and concrete examples, demonstrating the impact of aligning your communication and leadership with core values. This book is a beacon of hope, illuminating a path to success that is both effective and deeply meaningful.

HUBERT JOLY, Former Best Buy CEO
Senior Lecturer, Harvard Business School
Author of *The Heart of Business*

Every day, I see how positive communication energizes people, from sharing bright spots, to storytelling, to just saying thank you. David Schreiner gets it. *Be the Best Part of Their Day* is a powerful statement on looking at the world through the lens of what's right rather than what's wrong. Right from his book's title, Schreiner reminds us of the difference we can make in people's lives when we choose to approach them with a mindset of abundance, appreciation, and love. I am grateful for David, his message, and his sincere desire to make healthcare better.

QUINT STUDER, Author of
The Calling: Why Healthcare Is So Special

David Schreiner successfully uses Appreciative Inquiry to effect robust communications in supporting the "how" of individual, team, and organizational change. This is an essential addition to any manager's tool kit. An essential book to read and, more importantly, to follow!

LEONARD SCHLESINGER,
Baker Foundation Professor, Harvard Business School

Read this book. It will be the best part of your day. Based on solid research and decades of experience as an industry-leading healthcare system CEO, Dave Schreiner's insights will fill you with joy, lift your leadership, and guide you in building an organizational culture in which people flourish and high performance becomes the norm. If you are a values-driven leader and want to supercharge your communication, this book is an essential read.

JIM LUDEMA, PHD, Dean, School of Business
Calvin University

In today's world of profound disengagement within the healthcare workforce, leaders struggle to make their organization financially viable; provide high-quality, safe care; and do so in a manner that is consumer-centric and focuses on improving the health status of their community. These goals are significantly more challenging in rural healthcare where recruitment and retention of physicians and other allied healthcare professionals have always been a daunting task.

Dave's thirty-year experience in serving Katherine Shaw Bethea Hospital and the Dixon, Illinois community is a testament to his "Servant Leadership" style where authenticity and moral and ethical decision-making represent the cultural foundation of his organization. He is never satisfied with the status quo and is always pushing for innovation and transformation of his health system. For him, the care rendered in his facility is as personal as in a small community: these are his friends, neighbors, fellow church members, and people for whom he cares deeply on a personal basis.

Dave's exemplary leadership style could have easily landed him in a larger community and larger health system, but he chose to commit his career to rural healthcare. One of his numerous accomplishments throughout his career was his selection to serve on the Board of Governors for the American College of Healthcare Executives. This is the premier association that represents more than forty-eight thousand healthcare executives in seventeen countries. What a great tribute to be selected among your peers to represent them on a national and international basis in such a prestigious position.

Dave is a wonderful husband, father, and mentor and is one of the most ethical and moral individuals I have ever met. I know the people who read this book will be inspired by his insight into what it means to be an authentic leader in today's challenging healthcare industry and beyond.

CHUCK STOKES, Past Chief Executive Officer
Memorial Hermann Health System, Houston, TX

This is a great read for any person in a leadership role—anyone trying to do good by enabling themselves and others to be at their best. David has done a masterful job in translating his own research on how CEOs in the healthcare industry operationalize a whole system stakeholder approach and appreciative leadership into practical and accessible behavioral tips for all leaders. It is important for leaders to note that this is not just another list of "to do's" or best practices from so-called "objective" surveys that currently crowd the popular management bookshelf. Having had the opportunity to work with David during his doctoral journey, I can attest to the fact that the advice and specific behavioral tips in this book come from real, lived experiences: his and his research subjects'. David "walks his talk" and humbly includes valuing his mistakes as learning experiences. His evolving wisdom about *being* a good leader is a gift to us all.

RON FRY, PHD, Chair and Chuck Fowler
Professor for Business as Agent of World Benefit
Case Western Reserve University

Be the Best Part of Their Day is a trusted blueprint that any leader should embrace in learning to communicate and relate with their teams. Truly an outstanding read. Dr. Schreiner lays out the playbook, packed with real-world examples, that will help anyone in leadership, professionally and personally!

HAYS WALDROP, Founder, Institute for
Healthcare Executives and Suppliers, Franklin, TN

Comprehensive leadership is theory + practice. Dave Schreiner has created a research-based look at leadership, balanced with his own unique executive perspective. Insights into appreciative inquiry, leadership theory, and effective communications are combined, so that the reader is better informed on how to create a culture of inclusion and caring.

CHRIS WESTFALL, Author of *Leadership Language* and *Easier*,
US National Elevator Pitch Champion

This book is a gem. David Schreiner has produced a book that every leader needs to read. As a result of his research and as a practicing CEO, David has identified clear differences between highly successful leaders and less successful leaders. The differences can be easily implemented, so this book is inspiring and extraordinarily useful for anyone who engages in leadership roles.

KIM CAMERON, William Russell Kelly Professor Emeritus of
Management & Organizations, Ross School of Business
Professor Emeritus of Higher Education
School of Education, University of Michigan

BE THE
BEST PART
OF THEIR
DAY

DAVID L. SCHREINER, PH.D.

BE THE BEST PART OF THEIR DAY

SUPERCHARGING COMMUNICATION WITH VALUES-DRIVEN LEADERSHIP

Advantage | Books

Published by Advantage, Charleston, South Carolina.
Member of Advantage Media.

ADVANTAGE is a registered trademark, and the Advantage colophon is a trademark of Advantage Media Group, Inc.

Printed in the United States of America.

10 9 8 7 6 5 4 3 2 1

ISBN: 978-1-64225-760-1 (Paperback)
ISBN: 978-1-64225-759-5 (eBook)

Library of Congress Control Number: 2023918576

Cover design by Matthew Morse.
Layout design by Lance Buckley.

This publication is designed to provide accurate and authoritative information in regard to the subject matter covered. It is sold with the understanding that the publisher is not engaged in rendering legal, accounting, or other professional services. If legal advice or other expert assistance is required, the services of a competent professional person should be sought.

Advantage Media helps busy entrepreneurs, CEOs, and leaders write and publish a book to grow their business and become the authority in their field. Advantage authors comprise an exclusive community of industry professionals, idea-makers, and thought leaders. Do you have a book idea or manuscript for consideration? We would love to hear from you at **AdvantageMedia.com**.

*To every leader who wakes up every morning
working to be the best part of someone's day.*

CONTENTS

INTRODUCTION

Wherever you go, there you are.

— BUCKAROO BANZAI

As the CEO of Katherine Shaw Bethea Hospital (KSB), a rural hospital in Dixon, Illinois, I run into the people our hospital serves in the course of my average day. I am a part of the community, which is one of the best parts of my job. In a place with a population of about fifteen thousand, it is not uncommon for me to go out for dinner with my wife and for people to approach me as the face of our community hospital.

Sometimes, that encounter is about a positive experience the person had at the hospital—perhaps how we took care of someone's elderly mom or dad, or delivered their baby, or they just had an encouraging encounter with a nurse or x-ray tech or doctor. But, of course, I also face the other side. Sometimes, especially in the current healthcare climate, as we all work within the sticky morass of insurance, budgets, and staffing, my dinner is interrupted by someone letting me know the hospital let them down in some way—a long wait, or a bill that was not itemized as it should have been, or a negative personal encounter with someone on staff.

Up until a few years ago, after three decades working at KSB, encounters like that would keep me awake at night. In some ways, I was not living up to my own expectations. But, because it's in my nature to serve and be proactive and positive, I wondered if there was some way to turn things around, to be able to make every encounter a better experience. No, I can't wave a magic wand, sprinkle pixie dust, and make insurance pay your claim (believe me, if I could, there'd be a pixie dust cloud in the air above our hospital), but I can try to ensure that you leave our encounter feeling cared about, treated with empathy and compassion, and "supercharged" with positivity around the nature of our communication/conversation. I decided that, at work, I wanted every employee or person in the hallways to feel that seeing me was the best part of their day.

Except I didn't know how to do that.

And I especially didn't know how to do that in the context of modern healthcare. However, I also knew my issues with communicating with my "constituents"—board members, physicians, patients/customers, executive colleagues, and hospital staff—were not unique. Every industry is looking for that edge in how they communicate. The best companies want to leave a positive imprint on the world. They want a brand that reflects their commitment to their consumers or their stakeholders, a place where people want to work, where they feel proud and energized by going into their workplace each day (or Zooming in, as we move some jobs to remote or hybrid).

The problem is, we use terms like "engagement" and "communications" with a very amorphous idea of what that means. Or how to excel at them.

In *Talent Engagement Quarterly*, Allan Church has written that the term "engagement" itself does not have a single, formal definition:

As a singular, aligned psychological construct and measurement model the answer to this question is an unequivocal NO. Today engagement is comprised of multiple

constructs and these continue to expand and evolve at
a seemingly endless pace. Companies continue to chase
the latest fads in this area and consulting firms are eager
to feed this need for novel and buzzworthy approaches.
Now, there probably is something legitimate in the concept
of engagement somewhere if we can agree to find it and
stick with it as a talent management profession. Why?
There is enough convergence in the literature that we can
argue there is something substantive to having employees
that are satisfied, connected, committed, productive,
supportive, and feeling positively linked to their jobs
and the company they keep. The problem comes when
it is time to define what we mean by engagement.[1]

Once we arrive at a definition of engagement or Supercharged Communications, how do we even measure it?

I remember feeling discouraged. Then I got lunch with Lee Murphy, PhD, who does some HR consulting for us. I consider him a mentor, and I told him, "I just don't feel like I'm succeeding. The metrics aren't moving. I'm … I'm not as excited as I used to be when I was a baby CEO, and I'm not sure what the right levers to push are."

He ended up telling me about the doctoral program he had gone through. He—quite excitedly—talked about the curriculum that emphasized leading self, leading teams, leading organizations, and leading communities. He also explained that if you don't have a firm understanding of what your values are and what's important to you, how can you expect to lead others? Thus "values-based leadership"

---

1   Allan Church, "Is Engagement Overrated? Five Questions to Consider Before Your Next Engagement Survey," *Talent Engagement Quarterly*, no. 9 (April 2016).

offers a chance to discover those values and then to turn around and use those values to inspire others.

When you get in that grind, the hamster wheel of ten- and twelve-hour days, and you're kind of working your way through the calendar, do you keep in mind what you're excited about and what the mission of the company where you work is? In my case, it's a hospital—a place vitally important to our rural community and the people in it. Along the way, I forgot that as the CEO, I can really spend my time anyway I want. At the end of the day, I am not making a widget. What I offer is my *time*. So how could I spend it best for the people of my hospital and community to thrive? If I am just kind of muddling through, then I'm not earning my money. More importantly, I'm not earning the right to lead our hospital.

The leadership doctoral program my mentor suggested was at a Catholic institution, Benedictine University. There was a didactic portion of it, and much of the program was about leading organizations and communities. After feeling a bit worn down and burned out in my position, I wanted to focus my energies again. After I was accepted to the program, I was suddenly reenergized in ways that—well, it will take this whole book to explain. More exciting, when it came time to plan for my dissertation, which I was urged to do early on, I gravitated toward the communications side of leadership.

I ended up interviewing CEOs at five of the best-performing rural hospitals in America, and I spent many hours examining the *data* behind Supercharged Communications (through research I designed myself). I realized that the results of my research would change my life and those of the people working in and around the hospital. But then I also realized it had applications everywhere. We are all leaders. How can we move through the world making a difference? I think I've found the formula, and I am excited to share it with my readers.

I hope, then, you will join me on this journey. This book is for you if you've wanted to discover the secret to making your communications transparent, honest, real, compassionate, inspiring—and supercharged. If you've wanted to invoke change and reach the people who matter most—then read on.

In every day, there are 1,440 minutes.
That means we have 1,440 daily
opportunities to make a positive impact.

—LES BROWN

THE BEST PART OF SOMEONE'S DAY

| *Communicating with Those Who Matter Most* |

What would you think if I told you I was going to give you the cheat code, between the covers of this book, that would make communication easier and more effective with the people that matter to you the most? Because isn't that what all leaders—what everyone—want? Here's what I very quickly realized as I took the deep dive into communication strategies and best practices. At its *core,* it's really about how people feel when they spend time with you. When that person leaves their meeting or encounter with you—is their day better?

I will give you an example. In the past, if someone came to me complaining that a bill was not itemized properly, and that they were frustrated by red tape, I would have absorbed their criticism and called billing to try to sort it. I'd make some vague reassurances (which I meant). But now it's different.

As you'll learn in this book, I approach situations like this totally differently. I now use Appreciative Inquiry.

Appreciative Inquiry (AI) is a "proven, collaborative, strength-based approach to facilitating positive change and building capacity in organizations, groups, and communities."[2]

Pioneered in the 1980s by David Cooperrider and Suresh Srivastva at the Weatherhead School of Management at Case Western Reserve University, the concept of Appreciative Inquiry involves leading by asking the right questions, and then carefully listening—as opposed to rushing in with a "solution."

So using our example of the bill someone is unhappy about, I listen. I pause. And then I start asking questions like:

If the bill looked EXACTLY as you want it to look, describe it to me in vivid detail.

What would you like to see on it?

I can tell you from experience, and from my research, as well as stories collected from colleagues, that this kind of communication style changes things in an instant. First of all, rather than inviting a laundry list of what is *wrong* with the bill, it invites specificity of what is needed for it to be *right. It switches our mindset from a deficit mentality to an abundance perspective.*

More importantly, it deflates the other person's cells, and it tamps down their frustration. They feel "heard." You are listening—and for many people that is all they want. In the healthcare professions, we are often meeting patients and their families at some of the most anxious and trying times of their lives. The global COVID pandemic really exacerbated that as well. I try to keep that foremost in my mind as I extend grace and plenty of compassion to them. It is about respect.

This concept was introduced to me by Jim Ludema, PhD, one of my professors as I worked toward my doctorate. It was a game-changer for me. By game-changer, I mean it profoundly improved

---

2   The Center for Appreciative Inquiry, "What is appreciative inquiry?," accessed February 16, 2023, https://www.centerforappreciativeinquiry.net/more-on-ai/what-is-appreciative-inquiry-ai/.

many aspects of my life, both personal and professional; it changed the way I look at almost every situation.

Appreciative Inquiry is obviously much more than an inquiry about a person mad about a bill. So, let's look at what's involved—and how it can impact the way you engage with the most important people in your life.

Who Are Your Constituents?

Who are the people who matter most to you in your current position? When I look around KSB, I see:

1. Patients

2. Their families and loved ones

3. The employees of the hospital at all levels—doctors, nurses, cafeteria workers, lab techs, nursing aides, *everyone* who works for us

4. Members of our executive team

5. Our board of directors

6. The community

I hope when you consider who your constituents are, who your stakeholders are, you do not just picture the board or department heads. Or the people who use your product and those who own stocks. While the world is a huge place, we all know it is also rather small. Whether through social media and other communications, or by simply leaving our footprint on the world as it impacts the people near us, it is an intimate place as well, and it's important to identify the people who, as my book title says, matter most.

Appreciative Inquiry: How Do You Do It?

At least for me, Appreciative Inquiry has become part of my DNA. It was a total resetting of the way I looked at communications.

When I did my research, my questions for the various health-care stakeholders were obviously geared toward my field. However, Appreciative Inquiry is something you can start right now, at this very moment, in whatever corporate (or personal) environment you are in.

The entire idea of Appreciative Inquiry is very much centered on that first word. According to the *Merriam-Webster Dictionary*, when you appreciate someone, you "grasp [their] nature, worth, quality [and] significance." You also "value or highly admire" them. You also "recognize [them] with gratitude."[3]

I don't know about you, but I have tossed the word "appreciate" around my whole life—and I don't know that I ever really understood the depth of caring invested in that word.

Then the "inquiry" part (which we will get into more deeply in this section) is based on asking questions with respect and *listening* (which we will also cover more extensively), following through, making sure that you truly understand the other person's concerns (not just "smile and nod"). Then, with that understanding, it's trying to see if there's a way that you can help them think through it or give them suggestions. However, you must also be open and willing to learn and hear new ideas. That latter piece is important, because you cannot supercharge communications when you start a conversation with "here's where you're wrong."

Depending on your personality, you may be the type of person who is a "fixer." You may—truly out of kindness or a sense of

---

3   Merriam-Webster, s.v. "Appreciate," accessed May 5, 2023, https://www.merriam-webster.com/dictionary/appreciate.

duty or respect—want to "fix" every problem that comes along. However, Appreciative Inquiry invites solutions, but it focuses on the inquiry and listening portions first. (We'll get into the aspects of real listening in chapter 2.)

I would like to take us through, in order, each piece or step to this Supercharged Communications approach. (You will see each part has a "D" word to represent it, as used by the Center for Appreciative Inquiry.)[4]

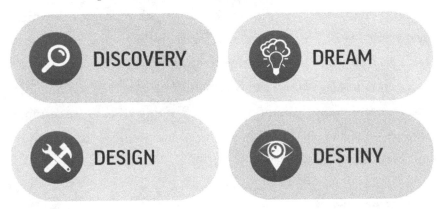

Definition

Before you approach a problem, you need to define it. However, you can define it as a negative or a positive. Just because there is a problem does not mean it has to be viewed through a negative lens. The first step is to frame your question in a positive way.

No: What is the chief complaint our emergency department is receiving?

Yes: When patients/families/the community have praised our emergency response team, when our team was performing at its best,

---

4   Center for Appreciative Inquiry, "The generic processes of appreciative inquiry," accessed February 19, 2023, https://www.centerforappreciativeinquiry.net/resources/the-generic-processes-of-appreciative-inquiry/.

what was the makeup of the team, environment of care, and teamwork atmosphere?

No: Why does our customer service department have longer call times than our competitors?

Yes: What are some of the positive aspects of our customer service department—when were we firing on all cylinders? What specifically makes our call center best in class?

As you can see, this "flips the script" to ask what your organization wants *more* of, as opposed to a focus on the problems you want to solve. You can tailor this to your industry, to your family even. Sometimes in life, we can feel bombarded by negatives, complaints, and frustration/anger/disappointment. Turning all these encounters around—reframing the problem in light of a positive—changes how you move through your day.

Discovery: Part 1

You have flipped the script. Your inquiry is down a positive rabbit hole—not a negative one. Now, you simply have to dig deeper into that positive. This involves interviews and collecting stories.

What does our community love about their hospital?

Why was our approach in the x-ray department so successful?

What makes our human resources department so exceptional?

What is working?

What should be celebrated?

We are all drawn to storytelling—in business and in our personal lives. It is how most of us engage with the world. In business, storytelling provides:

- A strong brand strategy, which enables stronger marketing.
- A way for a company to seem more human.

- A competitive advantage. Whose stories are more compelling?
- A connection between your constituents (those people who use your product or service, stakeholders, etc.) and reminds people of your organization's history and impact.[5]

Those are all compelling reasons, but it is the *human* element that especially interests us with Appreciative Inquiry.

I see it in healthcare, but I also see it all around. While statistics and data are important in tracking results and efficiencies, as well as key performance indicators (KPIs), when we hear a story that shows the positives in action, that's what we connect with. While most people won't remember that "World's Greatest Hospital" has performed two hundred heart transplants, has a waitlist patient count of xyz, and has outcome predictions of abc, they *will* remember a story about a young child being given the gift of life through the hospital because of a transplant, along with inspiring stories of the team that made that possible.

Questions for this portion of Appreciative Inquiry might include:

- When are we at our best as an organization?
- What are the stories that show that? Share the details and tell us more!
- What are the elements in place in those stories?
- When we're operating on all cylinders, what do you notice?

These stories can energize your constituents. By building on the positive, people can feel an excitement or a hopefulness—far more than stats, bar graphs, and a lot of internal "jargon-speak" can inspire.

5   Celline Da Costa, "Why every business needs powerful storytelling to grow," *Forbes*, December 19, 2017, accessed February 15, 2023, https://www.forbes.com/sites/celinnedacosta/2017/12/19/why-every-business-needs-powerful-storytelling-to-grow/?sh=50f403d643b0.

Life-Giving Forces: Discovery Part 2

Appreciative Inquiry uses a term called life-giving forces (LGFs). These are the "elements and experiences that represent the organization's strengths when it is operating at its very best."[6]

As the name implies, LGFs are those elements that should be nurtured, developed, and grown. *They give us life, therefore we should care for them and treasure them.*

I will give you an example from our hospital. I am sure there is not a person reading this book who has not gone to a large hospital, asked where a patient's room is, and been told by the person at the visitors' desk, "OK, walk down that long hall. Pass the first set of elevators, then make a left. Walk about halfway down and take the second corridor on the right. When you come to the next set of elevators, go on up to the seventh floor. When you get off the elevators, make a left, go past the MRI waiting room, and then take the third right, walk down that hall, and you will see the nurses' station."

At KSB, a visitor's experience is more likely to be, "It's right down that way to the elevator, but let me walk you there and make sure you get where you need to be."

KSB is known for the motto, "It's the People." And if I had to describe the special sauce that makes us a terrific community hospital, that's a big part. The excellence of our people.

Dream

The next part of Appreciative Inquiry is taking these positives and creating a dream or vision. In keeping with the earlier theme of connecting to stories, the dream should not be a list of KPI targets (not that those aren't important). Instead, it should include:

---

6   Center for Appreciative Inquiry, "The generic processes of appreciative inquiry."

1. Visual images

2. Word images

You might think of it as those vision boards many people create. You want to really *feel* the vision. This is very far different from a mission statement. Though KSB has one, this dream is much more on a deep, feeling level. Additionally, it should include what the Appreciative Inquiry technique calls Provocative Proposition. This means it looks at the positives of the NOW with the possibilities of the FUTURE. Building on what makes your organization great, what could it become?

"Faith is taking the first step even when you don't see the staircase." **—Martin Luther King, Jr.**

"If you dream it, you can do it." **—Walt Disney**

"We gain strength, and courage, and confidence by each experience in which we really stop to look fear in the face... we must do that which we think we cannot." **—Eleanor Roosevelt**

These sorts of lofty statements paint pictures with words. In this book, you will learn how to do the same for those around you.

Design and Destiny

I'm willing to bet most people in corporate America have been a part of some kind of process improvement committee. Maybe you have been tasked with finding solutions to a problem at work, and then to present the ideas you and your colleagues have come up with to those higher up in your organization or the C-Suite itself, or if you are a CEO, to your board.

Then what happened? Sometimes nothing. Sometimes just a logjam that stops any progress at just halfway, if that.

There are few things more frustrating than working feverishly on a problem or a vision, to channel real solutions, to come to a consensus with your peers and colleagues on the best course, and then to see those ideas aren't acted upon. However, in Appreciative Inquiry, this is when the real work begins.

Once everyone is on board, there should be energy within the organization for this new dream. How can innovation be inspired to make this a reality? What can be done to improvise and embrace the new future for your company, healthcare system, or nonprofit?

Along the way, your culture should be embracing these new Appreciative Inquiry competencies. The system should be changing for the positive. And, with the way Appreciative Inquiry focuses on the positive, successes should be celebrated.

I'm On Board, How Do I Do This?

When I speak on this topic, I am usually approached by someone afterward who says, "Great, sign me up. How do I use these practices in leadership?"

I am excited to share with you some of the best principles and concepts I have devised, learned from my studies and others, observed, and embraced. We'll spend the book examining just how to super-charge our engagement and how to measure the results.

One thing to share, before we move on, is I tried to use a cascading method. When I saw how this was a life-changing approach to leading, I was raring to go.

However, one criticism I received was: "This is just the flavor of the week." I think that's a fair concern when someone wants to jump right in and change the world. So, I decided to be very intentional. Whenever I came back from a seminar during my PhD journey, despite being so excited to share what I was learning and discovering with my research, I did not come in the next day with a long list of what we were going to do now.

Mahatma Gandhi is often credited with the saying, "Be the change you wish to see in the world." His actual quote is a little more involved, but the idea is the same. If we want to institute change, we must start with ourselves. I decided to embody this approach to leadership first. I needed to do it myself, to walk the walk, not just talk the talk. From there, I wanted it to cascade down. The way our organizational chart is laid out, there's me and five vice presidents, and then there is the department level (e.g., our ICU director or housekeeping director). I planned to spend several months with my administrative team on this before I even allowed myself to take it out at all to our management team.

"We but mirror the world. All the tendencies present in the outer world are to be found in the world of our body. If we could change ourselves, the tendencies in the world would also change. As a man changes his own nature, so does the attitude of the world change towards him. This is the divine mystery supreme. A wonderful thing it is and the source of our happiness. We need not wait to see what others do." **—Mahatma Gandhi**

Recap . . . and What's Next

I hope you are feeling a nascent excitement and hope for what this process and philosophy can do for your organization.

To recap:

1. Identify your constituents. *All of them.*

2. Remember that Appreciative Inquiry embraces true appreciation, compassion, and grace toward others. It also requires reframing your inquiries from negative to the positive.

3. Remember your D's: Definition; Discovery; Dream; Design; and Destiny.

4. Words and visions, *stories*, will captivate and inspire more than a lot of data and graphs.

5. When instituting changes, culture can be stubborn to transform. Start with yourself and cascade it out.

Next, we'll look at what "values-based leadership" really encompasses.

2

Never doubt that a small group of thoughtful,
concerned citizens can change the world.
Indeed it is the only thing that ever has.

—MARGARET MEAD

VALUES-BASED LEADERSHIP

Leading the Way, Making a Difference

Values-based leadership, especially as applied to engagement with your constituents (the people you care about, the people who rely on you), is more than a buzzy expression. It's a way of not just leading but living.

According to Benedictine University, where I studied for my PhD: "Values-driven leadership implies a conscious commitment by leaders at all levels to lead with their values and create a corporate culture that optimizes financial performance, ethical practice, social contribution, and environmental impact."[7]

By the time I finished my PhD, I realized that I definitely had a "conscious commitment" to lead with the values I believed in most. But I also knew that by my nature, and the nature of my job, I could go into "CEO mode"—looking at numbers and taking care of problems without fully connecting with the people involved. Being so solutions-focused means I entered into that C-Suite tunnel vision that can sometimes happen.

This is where Appreciative Inquiry is intertwined with values-driven leadership. Appreciative Inquiry opens the door to listening (actually

---

7   Benedictine University, "Values-driven leadership framework," accessed March 24, 2023, https://cvdl.ben.edu/leadership-framework/#:~:text=Values%2Ddriven%20 leadership%20implies%20a,social%20contribution%20and%20environmental%20impact.

hearing what is said) and keeping an open heart and mind (asking the types of questions that create positive engagement and connections).

What Are Your Values?

Everyone's values are not the same. Most of the time, there are themes and traits that emerge and are somewhat universal. At Benedictine, life-affirming values cited include:

HONESTY	INTEGRITY	EXCELLENCE
COURAGE	HUMILITY	TRUST
CARE FOR PEOPLE	SOCIAL RESPONSIBILITY	ENVIRONMENTAL RESPONSIBILITY[8]

Some people might add service, or passion, or other elements that feel core to them as *people*.

How Do You Lead?

Once someone commits to values-based leadership, then the way they lead needs to *align* with that. What do I mean?

Values must be lived and be a seamless part of how you operate as a leader.

I'll give you an example. I was interviewing someone for a director position. On paper, this person had a check next to every single box of what we were looking for professionally. In my office, this person had a megawatt smile and a positive attitude.

---

8   Ibid.

However, after they left I did what I always do. I asked the people who manned the reception desk, as well as my administrative assistant, "How were your interactions with this person?" Because it is one thing to be nice to the guy who can give you the job—but how do you treat the people you encounter from the moment you walk in the building?

The candidate had apparently been snappish over the previous night's lodging. He complained about the front desk staff and house-keepers. He was not friendly or even particularly polite to the KSB employees he encountered. Yet these were the *very same people* he would be working with each day.

We did not continue discussions with him.

In my mind, there was little point. Our KSB motto is "It's the People." And if you don't start with your values by recognizing that simple fact, you would not be at home in our hospital.

This commitment to values must then be reflected in your leadership—in your *actions*. Otherwise, these values can end up being like a mission statement, which is often an amazing, aspirational vision—but can feel rote.

"For me, I am driven by two main philosophies: know more today about the world than I knew yesterday and lessen the suffering of others. You'd be surprised how far that gets you." **—Neil deGrasse Tyson**

Values-driven leadership can be seen reflected in numerous big and small ways. One larger way, as an example, is communications. We will really explore this later in the book. However, for purposes of our briefer discussion here, think of what values-driven communications is—and what it isn't.

For instance, no human being anywhere should find out they lost their job via a tweet. Yet we have seen leaders do precisely that.[9] *Communications need to be transparent.* They also need to reach people where they are—in ways that work for them. At KSB, they might log onto our website and view a video communicating the latest hospital news and positive feedback; for someone else, it might be an email. I even give every new employee my cellphone number—it is very rarely used, but it's there if someone has something urgent they need to communicate with me about.

In terms of those communications and all interactions, we lead with trust and we lead with respect. I don't care if someone mops our floors—they are vital to what makes our hospital run—or is a top-earning physician. They are accorded the same level of appreciation, listening, and respect. I might, obviously, communicate with our chief nursing officer at the hospital about patient engagement scores and the director of housekeeping about linens or safety measures during COVID, but we're all equal and I offer the same depth of concern for both. Why wouldn't I?

Your Life Tree

When I was at Benedictine, a professor, Dr. Gus (James) Gustafson, utilized a tree to depict the concepts of values-based leadership (Figure 2.1). When I set out to write this book, I originally intended to provide my own tree here—and provide a blank one. However, while I am still putting mine here, with complete transparency (this is *really* mine—and I really do refer to it and update it three or four times every year), I decided to put the blank one in the last chapter. It's my

---

9   Jaclyn Diaz, "Fired by tweet: Elon Musk's actions are jeopardizing Twitter, experts say," *NPR*, November 17, 2022, accessed March 15, 2023, https://www.npr.org/2022/11/17/1137265843/elon-musk-fires-employee-by-tweet.

sincere hope that this book will give you food for thought and that your tree might look different by the time you reach "the end." (And it really won't be the end, but perhaps a new beginning.)

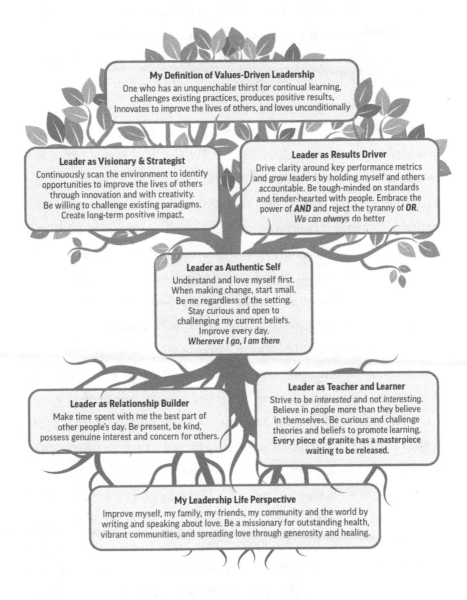

My Definition of Values-Driven Leadership
One who has an unquenchable thirst for continual learning, challenges existing practices, produces positive results, Innovates to improve the lives of others, and loves unconditionally

Leader as Visionary & Strategist
Continuously scan the environment to identify opportunities to improve the lives of others through innovation and with creativity. Be willing to challenge existing paradigms. Create long-term positive impact.

Leader as Results Driver
Drive clarity around key performance metrics and grow leaders by holding myself and others accountable. Be tough-minded on standards and tender-hearted with people. Embrace the power of **AND** and reject the tyranny of **OR**. *We can always do better*

Leader as Authentic Self
Understand and love myself first. When making change, start small. Be me regardless of the setting. Stay curious and open to challenging my current beliefs. Improve every day. *Wherever I go, I am there*

Leader as Relationship Builder
Make time spent with me the best part of other people's day. Be present, be kind, possess genuine interest and concern for others.

Leader as Teacher and Learner
Strive to be *interested* and not *interesting*. Believe in people more than they believe in themselves. Be curious and challenge theories and beliefs to promote learning. **Every piece of granite has a masterpiece waiting to be released.**

My Leadership Life Perspective
Improve myself, my family, my friends, my community and the world by writing and speaking about love. Be a missionary for outstanding health, vibrant communities, and spreading love through generosity and healing.

Figure 2.1 The Life Tree of values-based leadership.
Adapted with kind permission from Dr. Gus (James) Gustafson.

Once you see how to create your own Life Tree, you will see it can be adapted for your personal life—and to that end, since our professional lives are so intertwined with the personal, particularly in the area of this kind of leadership, you will see that intersection in my tree. However, let's view mine from the perspective of values-driven leadership. I'll go through the seven areas of the tree here. In addition, for each, I will pose some questions through the lens of Appreciative Inquiry.

My Definition of Values-Driven Leadership: As I said earlier in the chapter, we all have different values set in terms of what we value—and how we "weight" those values. By that I mean, for example, I know a woman who values loyalty and kindness over all other values—loyalty is extremely important to her. Someone else might weight environmental responsibility and stewardship as well as pursuing excellence in that highest spot. Diversity and inclusion is another value many want to strongly commit to and emphasize. However, this box is really about defining values-based leadership itself—what sort of "impact statement" would you make in that box? To help you (and to demonstrate how Appreciative Inquiry works here), you might ask: If you were picking the one thing that is most important to your leadership style, when you were operating at the top of your game, what would that one thing be? Define it for yourself. Then what does that mean to you? If you exhibited that leadership in a meeting, a conversation, a presentation, or a paper, what would that look like?

Leaders as Results Drivers: As a CEO, at the end of the day, I need to get results—a hospital and all the people it affects are counting on me to deliver leadership. What does that mean to you? Imagine you come out of a meeting with someone, or you gave a presentation, and in that moment, you realized you really met your own definition of leader as results driver. What would that look like? As you can see on mine, I advocate being tough on standards but tender-hearted with people. I am a CEO—and values and Appreciative Inquiry are about supercharging engagement—but at the same time, I have a board to report to, I have constituents counting on me, I have patient and public safety to be concerned about, and I have a community that needs our organization to be strong. I cannot compromise on safety standards, for example. I care about KPIs and want to see them met. But I remain compassionate with the people doing the work and making the magic happen.

Leader as Teacher and Learner: Part of Appreciative Inquiry is remaining a lifelong learner. If you go into any situation or conversation thinking you are all-knowing, I can promise you that you will not be the best part of *anyone's* day. In my Life Tree, I also want to be a good teacher—and recognize the worth of everyone I encounter. As attributed to Michelangelo (and paraphrased in a variety of ways), in every block of marble is a masterpiece that just needs to be uncovered. I *love* looking for that masterpiece in every human being. How do we work together to put ourselves in a position to be successful? Because if we're successful, then our organization is successful.

The Appreciative Inquiry way would be to ask, if I were leading as mentor, as teacher, as colleague, what would that look like? Think back to a time when you knew you knocked it out of the park as far as teaching someone—what did that feel like? What were the factors that made it so? By the way, I used to, at organizational meetings, dominate the conversation as CEO. During my PhD program, I learned I really should—as leader, teacher, *and* learner—be listening 75 percent of the time! For this box, think of a time when you contributed to the development of others through appreciative questions. Through listening and learning.

My Leadership Life Perspective: As I mentioned earlier, this tree can be adapted to . . . life. To whom you want to be as a person, as part of the fabric of the world. My challenge to myself with this tree is to constantly try to improve myself, my family, my community, and the larger world.

If we were sitting here a year from now and I were evaluating you (I realize you don't work with me—but you get the idea), what would I say about the values you brought to the workplace?

Do you have the consistency in your mindset to be able to take the things that are most important to you and reiterate them time after time, and find creative new ways to do that in today's environment?

The question about life perspective is that if you had the opportunity to have the people that are closest to you define what is most important to you, what they think you stand for, what would that be?

Leader as Relationship Builder: This is really about how you interact with people. What do you want to bring to every encounter with you? You want to be the best part of someone's day. You want to be "present" and real and caring. In terms of Appreciative Inquiry, ask yourself, "When was a time when I really connected to someone during my day?" Describe what made that encounter so positive. How did you behave? How did you feel as you made that connection? What did that person tell their partner when they got home and described the interaction?

Imagine if, as a person in the C-Suite or a leader, as soon as you walked out of a meeting, the people in attendance gave you a tip—a gratuity at the end, like they do servers. Would they give you a 5 percent, 10 percent, or 20 percent tip?

Change Leader: Good leaders are agents of change where it's needed. To examine this in an Appreciative Inquiry way, if you were looking at your organization's key metrics and you were able to be in the outstanding category in every one of them, what would that look like? What would you have to do? What philosophy, what attitude would you need to bring in order to be that successful? What unique philosophy do you bring to introduce and hardwire change?

Just because Appreciative Inquiry and values-driven leadership have a people-focused approach—a values approach—does not mean there are no KPIs that you cannot measure how it works.

Leader as Authentic Self: This is the consistency in the way that you show up in the world. Some of us have to work on this, perhaps because of imposter syndrome, or because we put up barriers to really getting to know us authentically. You have to love yourself enough to realize you are enough.

Another way that I try to look at this is if I show up as my authentic self and that's not well received by someone, that's OK. It is perfectly fine if someone doesn't care for me—and it does not have to ruin my day or make me change. I do not need to be fearful of being authentic.

My Appreciative Inquiry question for this is how do you show up in a consistent way? What does it look like at times when you showed up in your own authentic way? How do you *feel* when you know you're being real?

You may adapt your tree—again, you might have other areas you want to explore as leader. But the main idea is to look at this as representing your whole of self as you move toward the best communication with those who are most important to you.

Recap . . . and What's Next

This chapter and the Life Tree has, I hope, given you an idea of how values-driven leadership can lead to both deeper connections and Supercharged Communications in your organization— and your life. Remember that values-based leadership requires a conscious commitment.

1. What is your definition of values-driven leadership?

2. As a leader, how are you a results driver?

3. What is your leadership role as both teacher and learner?

4. What is your leadership life perspective?

5. In what way are you a change leader?

6. Describe your most authentic self.

Next, we'll pull back the curtain a little and show you the work that led me to the actionable elements of Supercharged Communications. I want to establish that this is all research-based. I promise the look at the research won't be painful at all. (Just like when the doctor tells you "this won't hurt a bit.")

When people talk, listen completely.
Most people never listen.

—ERNEST HEMINGWAY

ARRIVING AT SUPERCHARGED PRINCIPLES OF COMMUNICATION

How to Engage in the Most Impactful Way Possible

Now, let me tell you about my research (I hear that collective groan—I promise, it's important and not boring)—and some of its results. By the end of the process of my dissertation, I realized there were three key areas that were essential to engagement—and in each of those areas, there were methodologies, real and practicable. These are methods you can introduce into your organization tomorrow. In addition, as I tell you about my own journey in chapter 4, you will discover that you can take the principles I distilled and use them in your life—with your partner, your children, your parents, and all the people in your life who matter to you, as well as people you engage with in your everyday life. I also found you cannot do just one Supercharged Principle. You need to do all three in order to get the best results. But more on that in a bit.

First, I wrote this chapter because I wanted to make clear that I didn't just pull these concepts out of thin air. I spent three years understanding and defining these principles. I set out to study—and *quantify*—what actually enhances engagement with the people most important to you and your organization.

A visionary and strategic leader continuously scans the environment to identify opportunities to improve the lives of others through innovation and creativity and is willing to challenge existing paradigms.

This chapter will give you a high-level overview of how, through my coursework and dissertation, I developed my new leadership practices. It's important, if you are in leadership, if you are a director or in the C-Suite, that you know where these concepts and principles came from. It will also demonstrate that this methodology can be quantified.

Or, more simply: *It works.*

What I Wanted to Study

In graduate school, as doctoral candidates, we were told we should decide what area we wanted to direct our studies toward early on. For some of us, that induced panic. However, I knew pretty early on that I wanted to study executive communication—how to improve it and how to supercharge it. I knew there had to be a better way, for me and others around me, to engage with our constituents. In my case, my constituents were my board members and my entire team—from the person manning the visitors' desk to our chief medical officer, from our amazing housekeeping team to our lab workers, as well as KSB Hospital and the people who work there. In addition, as a rural hospital, we are very much part of the community we serve.

To give a simple example, members of our staff often visit our local schools, not only to essentially plant seeds of recruitment and outreach ("Hey, one day, you might want to be a nurse, doctor, or work for us!") but also to reach kids with messaging on opioid use or healthy living. In Dixon, Illinois, where we are located, we are so much a part of the community that it is impossible not to know someone who doesn't have an immediate family member, best friend, cousin, or casual acquaintance—or some combination of "six degrees of separation" of connection—to the hospital.

I wanted to increase engagement in all these constituent areas—not just for me but also for my team. I like to use this definition of engagement: "A connection to one's work characterized by dedication, vigor, and absorption."[10]

Engagement in the workplace enhances the culture, it increases productivity, it unites everyone with a mission or vision, it reduces absenteeism, and it generates an improved bottom line—whether that's financials/profit or KPIs, increased employee engagement, and greater customer engagement.

The purpose and title of my research were to explore what CEO practices help rural hospitals engage constituents in these volatile, uncertain, complex, and ambiguous times.

If I am honest, I was looking to recharge my own engagement.

How I Designed the Study

There is a risk, when you talk about concepts like communication and engagement that it can be too amorphous. It's difficult to wrap your arms around. So here are a few of the specifics of my research. I include them because regardless of your industry or organization, this will give you food for thought as far as establishing your own concepts and metrics.

---

10   Sandhya Rao et al., "Physician Engagement and Career Satisfaction in a Large Academic Medical Practice," *Clinical Medicine & Research* 18, no. 1 (2020): 3–10.

The Focus of My Study

First, I chose to study my own sector. I wanted to find out what other rural hospitals were doing—what worked, and what didn't. I started with defining rural hospitals, using the Lown Institute Hospitals Index to narrow down my definition. According to this index, America has 281 rural, "tweener" hospitals. Now, most people think of tweens as fourth and fifth graders on their way to middle school. But in the world of hospitals, tweener hospitals are just what that sounds like. We're not the big city academic medical center, or one with five hundred beds or more. And we're not a critical access hospital, which are very small hospitals that receive federal support in order to ensure that the rural areas have access to the healthcare they need (to receive the critical access hospital designation, there are criteria, including that they have no more than twenty-five inpatient beds).[11]

Why I Chose to Study the Challenges in My Industry

Rural hospitals suffer from some of the same challenges as the communities they serve. According to Pew Research, from 2010 to 2020, rural America lost about a quarter of a million inhabitants.[12] The population in small towns is shrinking and aging. The reasons include shrinking birth rates as the next generation puts off starting families, young people moving to more urban areas for opportunities, economic downturn, and suburban creep.

---

11   Centers for Medicare & Medicaid Services, "Certification and compliance for critical access hospitals (CAHs)," accessed March 24, 2023, https://www.cms.gov/Medicare/Provider-Enrollment-and-Certification/CertificationandComplianc/CAHs.

12   Tim Henderson, "Shrinking rural America faces state power struggle," *Pew Research*, August 10, 2021, accessed March 12, 2023, https://www.pewtrusts.org/en/research-and-analysis/blogs/stateline/2021/08/10/shrinking-rural-america-faces-state-power-struggle.

In addition, the nationwide transition from inpatient care to outpatient services harms rural hospitals. Outpatient ancillary services, such as medical imaging and physical rehabilitation, often draw patients with better insurance. For example, where Dixon is located, oftentimes people will travel to Chicago for certain treatments, tests, or surgeries. Alternatively, they may go to a larger hospital in a suburb elsewhere. Inpatient volume is migrating to the outpatient setting for rural hospitals, resulting in decreased reimbursement. Keeping the proverbial lights on is getting more and more difficult for many rural hospitals. The global COVID pandemic only worsened that.

America's rural hospitals are a foundational cornerstone of small communities—we are important to the fabric of life (something we'll talk about later in the chapter). In my community, our beautiful hospital is nestled in a walkable neighborhood of craftsman homes overlooking a picturesque river. A drive through our town has the elements of a Hallmark channel movie—from the beautiful theatre to restaurants where you can eat amazing meals by local chefs. We at KSB are there for the people of this town and the areas beyond it.

Some of the most critical moments in our lives happen in hospitals; babies are born, emergency care is delivered, and sick people are treated—and sometimes supported as they die. Hospital closures in rural communities cause delays in receiving care because of increased transportation times. If a patient must travel thirty minutes in an urgent cardiac crisis, that can literally be the difference between life and death. In addition, patient outcomes are improved by having visitors—and if a patient is further from home, that makes visits more problematic.[13]

---

13   Shiva Kaleghparast et al., "A Review of Visiting Policies in Intensive Care Units," *Global Journal of Health Science* 8, no. 6 (June 2016): 267–276, https://www.ncbi.nlm.nih.gov/pmc/articles/PMC4954899/.

When hospitals close, rural communities realize a significant negative economic impact, as well. As I said, in our community, we all know someone who works at KSB. Hospitals are often among the top two to three employers in rural areas. But other jobs leave when hospitals close their doors. Related industries—such as food and banking, construction, and restaurants—suffer.

My own commitment to my constituents meant I wanted to be part of a solution to these problems—and I knew I wanted to address some of that in the form of engagement, how we were doing and how we could improve (and how I as a CEO could improve).

If you are a sales leader, you will have your own challenges and markers of how you are doing on engagement. (We'll look at what I measured shortly—you will have different KPIs—but the principles behind Supercharged Engagement are the same.)

The Lown Institute Hospitals Index (2020) is a recent entry into the hospital ranking space. This ranking's uniqueness is the inclusion of how well hospitals serve people of lower income or education and people of color. Fifty-four metrics are distributed across four tiers. I decided to utilize this index in understanding how KSB was doing. I adapted one of their graphics for my own situation (Figure 3.1).

Figure 3.1 Adapted from Lown Institute Hospitals Index metric distribution.

Leadership Challenges, Industry Challenges

Leaders must lead through the easy times, the times when a company or organization is doing well, hitting all their KPIs, and running like a well-oiled machine. And they must also lead through the challenges. It is in those challenges that the mettle of a leader is tested. Your industry may be facing supply chain issues (we have that too), personnel issues, market changes, and more. We had huge challenges—as did everyone in the healthcare sector—during the COVID pandemic.

The American College of Healthcare Executives conducts an annual survey asking what the top issues are that hospitals are confronting today. Their 2022 cited issues include:

- Financial challenges
- Workforce issues, personnel shortages
- Behavioral health/addiction issues
- Government mandates
- Patient safety and quality
- Access to care
- Patient satisfaction
- Physician–hospital relations
- Technology
- Population health management
- Reorganizations (including mergers and acquisitions)[14]

I might add to that, because of the COVID crisis, there were also extraordinary and increased demands on healthcare and rampant employee burnout, particularly in front-line workers, but truly for

---

14   American College of Healthcare Executives, "Top issues confront-
      ing hospitals in 2022," accessed March 28, 2023, https://www.ache.org/
      learning-center/research/about-the-field/top-issues-confronting-hospitals/
      top-issues-confronting-hospitals-in-2022.

everyone in the hospital. People were coming to work—whether that was to work as an x-ray tech or a housekeeper or a nurse or an orthopedic surgeon—and they were rightly worried about catching COVID, and they were rightly concerned about bringing it home to their own families. In addition, healthcare workers were overwhelmed by the number of deaths and the influx of very, very sick people.

Healthcare systems also struggle to adjust to the demands of a more competitive, resource-scarce, and volatile environment, and lack of trust in leaders has been cited as an essential barrier to hospital improvement efforts.[15] I knew (or was hoping at the time) that what I uncovered in my research would help leaders gain and earn the trust of their constituents. *I* wanted the trust of my constituents. I hoped that I could figure out the "secret sauce" of engagement.

A rural hospital leader has the opportunity to interact with a Harvard-trained surgeon at a 9:00 a.m. meeting and a GED-educated housekeeper at 9.30 a.m. And both meetings can be of equal importance. As a CEO, I spin many plates and so do my fellow hospital executives. Engagement improvements had to cut through all the "noise" and engage everyone where they are.

So let me cut to the chase. I interviewed rural hospital CEOs, hospitals that were high-performing, in an attempt to dig into the secrets of engagement. I knew, too, that true engagement does not occur without Supercharged Communication. In simplistic terms, it's the difference between a conversation where the other person mutters yes or no answers, or shrugs, or acts disinterested (perhaps the typical conversation when you ask your teen how was school and they say "fine")—and being seated next to a brilliant conversationalist at a dinner party.

Communication is everything.

---

15   Clinton O. Longenecker and Paul D. Longenecker, "Why Hospital Improvement Efforts Fail: A View from the Front Line," *Journal of Healthcare Management* 59, no. 2 (2014): 147–157.

How Might Leaders Engage?

I looked at a number of different leadership styles. You may be familiar with servant leadership, transformational leadership, and even authoritarian leadership (you know—the "my way or the highway" CEO). The leadership styles I studied in depth included authentic, servant, socially responsible, and positively energizing leadership. I also looked at the most high-performing rural hospitals and ascertained the leadership styles there.

Authentic Leadership

The first type of leadership I analyzed was authentic leadership.

> Authentic leadership emphasizes that being an effective leader entails high self-awareness and demonstrating consistency between one's values and actions. Leaders and followers have to share a high sense of transparency so that both leader and follower understand the other's preferences, values, and emotions.[16]

I think we all aspire to be authentic. On a personal level, think about someone you feel is "fake." They smile at you, but you know they are actually saying things behind your back—or you can see the disinterest in their eyes when you are speaking to them. That is a big negative. Do you walk the talk? Are you consistent? Authentic? Are your personal and professional values reflected in all your interactions?

---

16   Marion B. Eberly, Michael D. Johnson, Morela Hernandez, Bruce J. Avolio, "An Integrative Process Model of Leadership: Examining Loci, Mechanisms, and Event Cycles," *American Psychologist* 68, no. 6 (2013): 427–443. https://doi.org/10.1037/a0032244.

You cannot earn your constituents' trust if who you are varies depending on who you are talking to—or even what day it is. If you "blow the way the wind blows," you are not being an authentic leader. With Supercharged Communication techniques, you will learn how to deepen your authenticity.

Discovering your authentic leadership values and style can be your life's work. Authentic leadership emerges from life stories, and personal, continuing development is a necessary component of growth (the idea of lifelong learning, as well as lifelong self-discovery). Authentic leaders use life experiences to form their values and reflect on them to determine their leadership style and actions.

For example, I am from rural America. Though I lived in an urban area for a couple of years, returning to rural America was always my plan. Rural America raised me—my values reflect a caring for the people of small towns, for rural farmers, for the generational families of my area, as well as the simple lesson of the Golden Rule. You treat people—regardless of race, religion, sexual orientation, or job title— the way you want to be treated.

I have heard and witnessed many front-line workers confronted with a "difficult" patient who may be saying unkind things to them or being disruptive. They react with remarkable patience. I recall a nurse telling me he treats every elderly patient how he would treat his own grandma. That is authenticity. These workers bring *who they are* and the values they hold dear to the hospital every single day. They showed up during COVID because of their commitment to their patients as well as their community. They more than walked the talk.

I'll give you another real-life example. We had a Friday evening, not all that long ago, when a dozen women were all having their babies at the same time. It happens, but I had never seen anything quite like it at our hospital. No sooner had the obstetric nurses settled a woman and her partner in a room that another showed up—and another. The doctors and nurses were running from room to room, I am sure praying some of those babies would wait a little bit longer.

We ended up putting out an urgent "SOS" call for anyone from the department, doctors, nurses, etc., who had the weekend off, to volunteer to come to work to get us through this remarkable baby extravaganza. It was a call for all hands on deck. And the response was incredibly gratifying. More than enough people showed up—and showed up cheerfully. It was the magic of teamwork in action, as well as that authentic commitment to the hospital and the people of Dixon.

Gardner et al. pointed out that developing followers is a crucial concern for the authentic leader:

Authentic leadership extends beyond the authenticity of the leader as a person to encompass authentic relations with followers and associates. These relationships are characterized by a) transparency, openness, and trust, b) guidance toward worthy objectives and c) an emphasis on follower development.[17]

The facets of an authentic leadership style overlap substantially with ideas popularized by the concept of emotional intelligence, which was first coined by Peter Salavoy and John Mayer in 1990.[18] Daniel

---

17   William L. Gardner et al., "'Can You See the Real Me?' A Self-based Model of Authentic Leader and Follower Development," *The Leadership Quarterly* 16, no. 3 (2005): 343–372. https://doi.org/10.1016/j.leaqua.2005.03.003.

18   Matthew Channell, "Daniel Goleman's emotional intelligence in leadership: How to improve motivation in your team," TSW Training, October 13, 2021, accessed March 15, 2023, https://www.tsw.co.uk/blog/leadership-and-management/daniel-goleman-emotional-intelligence/#:~:text=Daniel%20Goleman's%20emotional%20intelligence%20theory,happier%20and%20healthier%20working%20culture.

Goleman expanded and expounded on the ideas and went on to examine it in a longitudinal study. In fact, Goleman considered emotional intelligence (emotional quotient or EQ) as perhaps more important than intellectual quotient or IQ. EQ is an important (and large) concept. So I will shorten to simply this: do you work and play well in the sandbox with others?

Servant Leadership

Servant leaders prioritize the greater good. Peter Northouse is a legend in the field of leadership, and I was fortunate to have him as a professor in my doctoral program. I even had the chance to pick his brain over breakfast a couple of mornings at our hotel. Dr. Northouse describes servant leadership as the *caring principle,* with leaders as servants who focus on their followers' needs to help these followers become more autonomous, knowledgeable, and like servants themselves.[19] Some of the world's leading corporations have adopted servant leadership practices, including Starbucks, Marriott International, SAS, and FedEx.[20] Servant leaders see themselves as stewards of the organizations. They are caretakers of the companies they are with, and they also see employee and follower development as part of their mission.

Authentic leadership and servant leadership are closely aligned. I examined this in the context of rural hospitals. When considering the context of leadership in rural medicine, authentic leaders and servant leaders conform nicely into the space. Authentic leaders need and take opportunities to interact with their constituents. Servant leaders view hospital leadership as an opportunity to serve multiple constituents.

---

19   Peter G. Northouse, *Leadership: Theory and practice,* 8th ed. (Sage Publications, Thousand Oaks, Ca. 2018).

20   SkillPacks.com, "7 Servant leadership examples to inspire and guide you," accessed March 27, 2023, https://www.skillpacks.com/servant-leadership-examples-in-business/.

Positively Energizing Leadership

Of the types of leadership I examined, this is probably the least well known. Kim Cameron, from the Center for Positive Organizations at the University of Michigan, was also one of my doctoral professors and a member of my dissertation committee. The lens through which Cameron views the world has had a dramatic impact on me. I've personally adopted many of his views. Dr. Cameron defined positively energizing leadership with this basic message: "All human beings flourish in the presence of light or of positive energy" (p. vii).[21] I looked for comments from constituents about positivity and negativity through the interviews conducted. I looked for examples of generosity, compassion, gratitude, trustworthiness, forgiveness, and kindness, all qualities mentioned in Cameron's work. How was engagement impacted if all or some of these traits were present?

Cameron described what he called an organization's *influence network* and the impact positively energizing leadership at the top of the organizational chart can have on the business: "Human beings are inherently inclined toward virtuous behavior; virtuous behavior is a key element in creating strong, flourishing relationships; and these relationships produce positive outcomes" (p. 5).[22] I attempted to connect the literature on flourishing relationships and draw a connection between acts that create a flourishing environment and organizational success.

Cameron concluded that positive energizers impact performance and exude a certain kind of light or an uplifting energy that helps others become their best. He identified attributes of positively energizing leaders such as *expressing gratitude* (remember this one because it

---

21   Kim Cameron, *Positively Energizing Leadership: Virtuous Actions and Relationships That Create High Performance* (Berrett-Koehler Publishers, Oakland, Ca. 2021).

22   Ibid.

is hugely important to Supercharged Communication), investing in relationships, listening actively, and genuine, authentic behavior by the executive (p. 57).[23]

The Secret Sauce

I was very excited when I thought I had figured out the recipe for engagement, the "secret sauce." Four themes or avenues of engagement emerge from the leadership theories I studied:

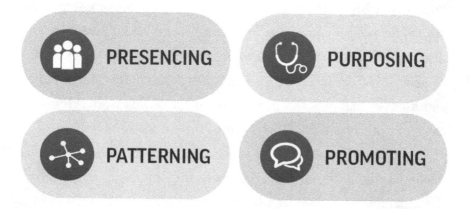

These themes guided the semi-structured interview questions I conducted with the chosen CEOs. Let's look at each theme in turn—these will start you thinking on the path to engagement.

Leadership Presencing—Engaging in the Moment

Leaders are "on stage" the moment they get out of their car at their workplace (and even where they park!). The words they say are magnified, and the actions they take are enriched and spread contagiously throughout the organization. The interactions experienced with team members greatly influence and shape organizational culture.

---

23   Ibid.

Consider the following example regarding Apple's Tim Cook. An Apple sales associate described his first impression of the company's CEO in a blog:

> For Tim Cook, there are no dumb questions.
> When he answered me, he spoke to me as if I
> were the most important person at Apple.
>
> Indeed, he addressed me as if I were Steve Jobs himself.
> His look, his tone, the long pause...that's the day I began
> to feel like more than just a replaceable part. I was one
> of the tens of thousands of integral parts of Apple.[24]

Being "present" has deeper meaning than being at your job, at a meeting, and listening to a presentation or even talking with your board. "Present" takes it to another level. If *your body* is in that meeting or that one-on-one—where is your mind?

We have all had the experience of having a very difficult personal situation and trying to function on the job. It may be an ill family member, a financial issue, an argument with a partner, a teen who is going through a rough time at home. We're "there" at our desks. But our heart, soul, and mind are somewhere else.

Being present, with practice, is a choice. It's a habit. And like any muscle, it gets stronger with repetition.

It is no accident that Buddhists call *Puja* a "practice," or why yoga teachers often refer to yoga as a practice. You can train yourself to be more fully present. In fact, mindfulness meditation and a commitment to mindfulness can transform you into a better leader.

---

24 Kristie Rogers, "Do Your Employees Feel Respected?" *Harvard Business Review*, July–August 2018, 62–72, https://hbr.org/2018/07/do-your-employees-feel-respected.

Rasmus Hougaard and Jacqueline Carter, authors of *The Mind of the Leader*, surveyed a thousand leaders, "who indicated that a more mindful presence is the optimal strategy to engage their people, create better connections, and improve performance."[25]

In another survey of two thousand employees, Bain & Company found that "among thirty-three leadership traits—including creating compelling objectives, expressing ideas clearly, and being receptive to input —the ability to be mindfully present (also called *centeredness*) is the most essential of all."[26] I have incorporated meditation into my daily routine, and I can vouch for its effectiveness.

I think of this in my own professional role—and invite you to think of it in yours, as well. When I enter KSB, I know my walk through the halls to my office might take twenty minutes. I try to greet, engage with, and truly connect with everyone I pass. It is informal, but it's important I be seen out and about and not be some guy in the corner office. I need to be *approachable*, and once approached, I need to offer my attention.

I also know that were I to park in my parking spot, charge in, eyes straight ahead, clearly in a rush, not even offering a smile to the patients, their families, the KSB employees, and so on, that I set a tone for my hospital—and it's not a good one.

In fact, I make it a point when I have a meeting with someone to poke my head out the door and tell my amazing administrative assistant "hold my calls." I like for the person I am in a meeting with to actually *hear* me say that, because it shows them how much I value their time with me. My name may be on my door, but I am no more

---

25   Rasmus Hougaard and Jacqueline Carter, "If you aspire to be a great leader, be present," *Harvard Business Review*, December 13, 2017, accessed March 16, 2023, https://hbr.org/2017/12/if-you-aspire-to-be-a-great-leader-be-present.

26   Ibid.

or less important than the people facing me. I also ensure that a desk does not separate us. I eliminate that physical barrier.

It is not only what the CEO's communication is about, it is about how it is delivered and how the leader's presence is experienced by other(s). CEOs—no matter the industry—tend to run at a frantic pace. Meetings, executive duties, administrative and fiduciary obligations, decision-making, and so much more. The other piece of it is obviously "the people." They will always be any company's greatest asset. As I mentioned before, I have to make sure I don't slip into CEO tunnel vision. Working on **presencing** is something I *practice* every single day.

Purposing—Communicating Vision and Values

A hospital, in many ways, has a higher calling to the patients and families they serve, to bettering their health through prevention and care. In my experience, most people go into medicine because they want to help people.

However, times have never been more uncertain. COVID has decimated rural hospitals and has taken a human toll. It is in times like these that employee engagement is more important than ever. It is also even more important to hear from leaders and for those leaders to convey vision and values clearly—the purpose that can unite everyone.

When you have a vision, it is like having a compass that points to True North. Everyone knows where we are collectively going.

Healthcare is not the only sector to have a "higher calling" and a vision. We see over and over, for example, young companies and start-ups driving toward creating something of value. Large companies from Apple to Marriott are often known for their enthusiastic culture. There is a "higher calling" to create the best product on the market or to offer a positive and memorable customer experience.

In the case of rural hospitals, CEOs and leaders are instrumental in impacting how their team members relate to the organization they serve. Employee engagement undoubtedly results in improved patient and community engagement. A study of registered nurses shows a favorable team-level experience is directly associated with patient engagement measured with vigor, dedication, and absorption constructs: "All work engagement dimensions were associated with job satisfaction, intention to stay in nursing work, and favorable ratings of quality of care on the unit."[27]

In today's uncertain, complex, and ambiguous times, many employees across all business sectors have an embedded level of anxiety about their organization's sustainability. Communication of the system's vision and values is imperative to build trust, which can help offset such anxiety.

Patterning the Fabric—Keeping the Organization Connected

Patterning is about weaving, connecting, or patterning multiple communications to provide a common or a shared sense of purpose, priorities, and directions. Communicative leadership suggests that all CEOs participate in continuous communication. But are they communicating competently?

As CEOs, we can be guilty of one-way communication—from us to them. It is as if our job is done once we hit the "send" button on the email or video. Unilateral, one-directional communication can be more uncomplicated and more comfortable for the busy CEO.

---

27   P. Van Bogaert et al., "Work Engagement Supports Nurse Workforce Stability and Quality of Care: Nursing Team-level Analysis in Psychiatric Hospitals," *Journal of Psychiatric and Mental Health Nursing* 20, no. 8 (2012): 679–686. https://doi.org/10.1111/jpm.12004.

Fire off an email or record a quick video and move on with the day. Bidirectional communication is more challenging.

A leader must also know that bidirectional communication means you may hear from people who aren't happy with something. In addition, bidirectional communication is vital for the other party to feel "heard"— whether they wish to express something positive or negative. That's where, I think, Appreciative Inquiry can transform that conversation.

In addition, a hospital represents a web of interdependent departments. Various specialties, the x-ray department, physical therapy department, pharmacy, and clinics, are part of the inner workings of a health system.

One interdepartmental relationship that in my own experience can have friction is between the emergency department (ED) and the medical/surgical floor. The ED regularly interacts with Med/Surg, and these interactions can be challenging. Discharging a patient from the ED to Med/Surg represents a win for the ED and more work for the staff on the medical/surgical units. An essential step in engagement is making sure one part of the organization knows what the other parts are doing, and that it all adds up to something coherent.[28] The leader is responsible for keeping all units interconnected and working toward common goals. A smooth transition between various settings—from physician office to ancillary testing to admission through discharge and even through the billing cycle— requires a connected organization.

You see this same issue in corporate America. For example, marketing may be responsible for building excitement about a product, and the salesforce must build their funnel. But what happens

---

28   Deborah Ancona, Elaine Backman, and Kate Isaacs, "Nimble leadership: Walking the line between creativity and chaos," *Harvard Business Review*, July–August 2019, 2–11, https://hbr.org/2019/07/nimble-leadership.

when they don't work in tandem? And then what if there is a surge in demand—but production has not kept up?

Shared meaning is essential for collaboration, and effective communication is critical in reaching shared meaning. It is more than making sure that messages are getting out, sent, and received. One-directional communication fails to deliver positive results. As George Bernard Shaw noted, "The single biggest problem in communication is the illusion that it has taken place."

Communication is enabled in a healthy, engaged way when leaders create trust and understanding. Team members need to see leaders in the hallways, cafeteria, and all departments and clinics. *You can't create a cohesive fabric as a leader if you are not one of the threads in that fabric.*

Promoting Positive Change

Even when you think you're communicating too much, you're probably not communicating enough.[29] (Later in the book, I will discuss the rhythm and frequency of communications, along with methods, in the section on communication mediums.)

The only constant in healthcare is change. New information technology results in systemic heartburn. Physician leaders starting and ending practices cause disruption, especially in rural hospitals where the physicians are well known (as I said, when my wife and I go out for dinner, inevitably someone will approach me, and the same is true for our doctors). Some patients prefer long-standing relationships with their physicians. When a physician leaves the community, the organization will attempt to redirect the patient to another doctor, often with mixed results based on the patient's preferences. A physician leaving the

---

29   Citrin, C. J., "The CEO Life Cycle," in *Reflections on Leadership and Career Development: On the couch with Manfred Kets de Vries*, ed. Mafred F.R. Kets de Vries, 184–200. https://doi.org/10.1002/9781119206477.ch9.

community also results in a negative financial impact from the loss of direct professional fees and the loss of ancillary revenue, such as medical imaging, laboratory studies, and physical therapy services.

When organizations are in the middle of significant change, senior managers may need to make top-down decisions, which, of course, flies in the face of collective decision-making. In this situation, it is more important than ever that leaders spend time explaining—and listening, with an emphasis on listening. Even so, some employees will resist the change, while others wish senior leaders would just "rip the Band-Aid off" and move decisively ahead. Facing such inflection points, change leaders (remember that from the Life Tree?) probably won't succeed unless they have previously established an excellent personal reputation within the firm—and the company has an equally good reputation with external stakeholders.[30]

Take a moment to consider whether your professional status keeps you from understanding that simple acknowledgment or praise from a leader is often enough to make an employee feel valued (Rogers, 2018).

Observations of a hospital CEO include the fact that healthcare is changing so quickly that if senior leaders are not out in front and doing the right things with their team and people, change efforts will fail, and the entire organization will fail (Chatfield et al., 2017).

My Approach

I chose to study the exemplars because of what I believe is a link to positive organizational scholarship. I focused on "A"-rated hospitals. I began at the top of the rankings. I worked my way through the listings until I successfully gained agreement from the CEO to personally

---

30   Ancona, Backman, and Isaacs "Nimble leadership."

participate in the study and allow people from within their organization to participate. I then worked with the CEOs' administrative assistants to make appointments with the CEO, the board chair, a physician, a senior executive, and an hourly employee. I attempted to research hospitals from various regions of the country. I interviewed the additional people aside from the CEO because sometimes there is a disconnect between what a leader thinks they are doing and conveying—and to recall our previous analogy—what those working closely with the CEO perceive.

I chose to study high-performing organizations (as defined by the Lown Institute Hospitals Index [2020]) further along on their engagement journey and operating in positive settings instead of struggling organizations. I decided not to compare and contrast the organizations but rather look for common themes or extraordinary practices contributing to constituent engagement.

I chose to conduct an extensive interview with the CEO, lasting between sixty and ninety minutes, to ensure enough time to build trust and rapport with the CEO and get all my questions answered. I wanted this to be a "conversation," the better to get deeper answers, as well as a stronger level of openness. I chose to conduct thirty-minute interviews with an executive, a physician, a board member, and a staff member. The CEO selected these other interview candidates. I requested that the staff member not be a member of the CEO's fan club but rather a representative of the larger employee population. The reason for multiple interviews was, again, to cross-check the CEO's statements and ensure the stakeholders actually experienced the CEO's behavior as the CEO described their practices.

The Appreciative Inquiry-designed interview questions invited interviewees to answer questions by recalling examples within their personal and organizational history in rich, vivid detail.

The Results

Once my interviews were completed, then the fun started (sort of). It was time to see what I had discovered. I found commonalities, and I started organizing them the old-fashioned way—with Post-It notes! (Figure 3.2).

I asked members of my executive team to place the notes in categories they found relevant. I used this team process to check (question) my perspective.

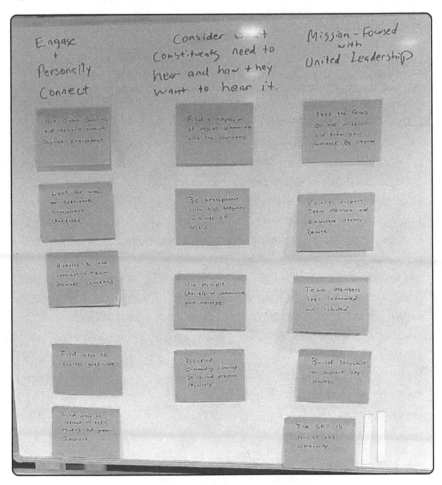

Figure 3.2 My organizational board.

In the end, I found three primary Supercharged Engagement Principles. Each then had five elements—practical, doable methods that actually work and that you and your team could start implementing right now.

The three Supercharged Engagement Principles are as follows:

1. Engage and connect at a personal level.

2. Engage with intent through various medium.

3. Be mission-focused through united leadership.

In each of the next chapters, we will focus on one of these areas, along with the five actionable engagement methods (seen in Figure 3.3).

SECOND-ORDER ENGAGEMENT CATEGORIES

Ask great questions and generate positivity	100%
Develop outstanding listening skills and practice them regularly	100%
Be accessible and show an interest in member concerns	100%
Finds ways to express gratitude	66%
Find ways to interact through rounding	100%
Find rhythm of regular communication with key constituents	100%
Be transport with high frequency	95%
Use multiple channels to communicate your message	90%
Look for ways to overcome engagement challenges	90%
In time of crisis, be intentional in communicating differently	90%
Keep the focus on the mission and know your audience -- be prepared	90%
Vocally support team members and encourage healthy debate	100%
Make team members feel informed and included	100%
Build structure to support key leaders	100%
The Executive is part of the community -- get involved	90%
Second-Order Confirmation Results	**94%**

Figure 3.3 The engagement categories.

The Life of a Leader

Before we move on, I had one more point I wanted to convey. I set out wanting to learn how America's best rural hospital CEOs engage with their constituents. I found driven, motivated, frustrated leaders who work long hours; sleep too little; capture, retain, and hold themselves responsible for a remarkable amount of intimate details; and keep fighting for their patients and employees. I could relate to their personal and professional challenges.

I spoke with board chairpersons, physicians, hospital leaders, and hourly employees, and they told me the respect they have for their CEO. They marveled at the CEO's work ethic, the hours invested, and the CEO's ability to be in multiple places at one time. The interviewees almost universally stated that they wouldn't want that person's job.

I know, for me personally, I cannot separate the stress and professional challenges from my true, values-based commitment to the people of my hospital and community. Knowing people come to a hospital from birth . . . through end-of-life . . . means I have a high calling. I am not making a widget (not that making widgets is not an honorable mission!). I am shepherding a hospital through today's challenges—and they are many.

You did it! You made it through the academic blah-blah-blah of a dissertation and still kept reading. Thanks for hanging in there. I promise it will get even better from here.

What do these executives have in common regarding their engagement practices, daily schedules, communication mediums, and styles? I think I have created a magic formula, and I am excited to share the details with you, starting with the next chapter.

Recap . . . and What's Next

I wanted my readers to know that the Supercharged Communication Principles I distilled down from my research is, indeed, research-based. We covered a lot in this chapter, but here are the highlights.

1. I set out to study CEOs at top-performing rural hospitals to get at the secrets of engagement. What I discovered were principles and methods that could be utilized across all sectors of business.

2. I shared the design and focus of the study, as well as who I interviewed, and my approach to those interviews.

3. Leadership challenges are always there for CEOs, and COVID was exceptionally challenging. For hospital CEOs, additionally, the life-and-death element of healthcare adds a layer of urgency.

4. I focused on three types of leadership: Authentic, Servant, and Positively Energizing.

5. I discovered the Four P's of CEO engagement: Presencing, Purposing, Patterning, and Promoting.

6. I ended up with three Principles of Supercharged Communication—along with fifteen specific, actionable methods.

Now, the next three chapters will do a deep dive into each of those principles and the methods specific to each one.

Thank you for continuing this journey to authentic engagement with me!

We have two ears and one mouth so that we can listen twice as much as we speak.

—EPICTETUS

SUPERCHARGED PRINCIPLE ONE

Engage and Connect at a Personal Level

I used to hide in my office.

I'm kidding—mostly. What I actually mean is as a new CEO, it was very easy to get lost in the thicket of numbers, the economics of running a hospital, and operational concerns. I thought my focus was to deal with various "issues" and so-called business fires that needed to be put out. It was easy to spend much of my time in my office—or at meeting after meeting. It was easy to spend a lot of time with our board of directors. I still find myself slipping into this practice on occasion.

But our hospital's very motto is "It's the people."

I am sure many in the C-Suite or any leadership position feel that familiar push and pull. But as I committed to Supercharged Communications and did my research, one of the first principles I discerned was: Engage and Connect at a Personal Level.

This essential principle includes five key parts (see Figure 4.1), which we will cover in detail in this chapter. Those elements are as follows:

1. Ask great questions and generate positivity.

2. Develop outstanding listening skills and practice them regularly.

3. Be accessible and show an interest in member concerns.

4. Find ways to express gratitude.

5. Find ways to interact through rounding.

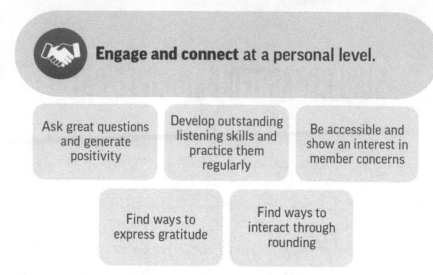

Figure 4.1 Supercharged principle number one.

We will cover each one, in turn. But one important thing before we move on. I no longer spend my time hiding in the weeds of numbers. I focus on engagement, and I am using all of the techniques we will cover in this chapter and the next two, in order to ensure that I am nurturing my team.

Ask Great Questions and Generate Positivity

You may recall from chapter 1 how important Appreciative Inquiry is to Supercharged Communications. We'll revisit it with this principle. Asking great questions of your team often includes having people think about when they were performing at their best. Phrasing your questions in an Appreciative Inquiry manner goes a long way in the workplace toward generating positivity. It *isn't* that you, as a leader, don't see your team's missteps or the problems in your organizations. It isn't burying your head in the sand or approaching it with trite phrases instead of real solutions. It *is*, however, about reminding people of their worth and reminding a team of the times when everything went *right*—and then chasing those results.

Asking great questions also means asking them of your customers, stakeholders, and, believe it or not, once this moves from a novel approach to a habit, the people in your life outside of work too. Asking great questions involves one very important trait: cultivating your curiosity.

> **Asking great questions involves one very important trait: cultivating your curiosity.**

Be interested.

Unfortunately, for many leaders, as we move up the corporate ladder, the tugs on our time that I mentioned at the start of the chapter grow more urgent. You may be thinking, *I don't have time to engage with so many people.*

I am here to tell you that generating positivity *depends* on your engagement. You don't have time *not* to engage with the people that matter to you the most. When I started my career, I knew the name of every single person I passed in the corridors of KSB Hospital. We had 350 employees then. Now, we have a thousand. As we grew and thrived, that became more difficult (I still try!). However, I still found that this interest and engagement was important enough that I could tailor it for a larger organization:

1. I have adjusted my schedule such that if I have to move through the buildings in order to attend a meeting, I allot an extra ten or fifteen minutes to get where I am going. This allows me to greet people, to chat with them, and (perhaps most importantly) to be

stopped in the hall because someone feels comfortable enough to approach me, knowing I welcome it.

2. While I cannot speak with everyone every day, I *can* ensure that when I am speaking with someone I am "present" and focused on them. I can ask them great questions—and I can demonstrate in how I interact with them that they are valued.

This principle has reinvigorated me to go to work every day—even after years at my job. It is super exciting because every time you stand in front of someone different in the workplace, you get to hear their story and learn more about them. Each encounter represents an opportunity to hear from the people closest to our patients (for you that might be your customers). When we have employee orientations, we start with introducing our executive team. Then, while we're all together, I have each employee go around and talk about themselves. Suddenly, that room is a bit smaller, and certainly warmer. That's the positivity piece.

By the way, practicing this will help *you* too. It's not just organizational mumbo jumbo. Shifting to this Supercharged Communications mindset will help you get "out of your head," for one thing. You'll also see your connections with your team deepen.

Don't know what to ask? Consider that Appreciative Inquiry and great questions will vary by situation. One-on-one questions can be general—everything from "how was your weekend?" to "how has your work–life balance been lately?" If you are a team leader meeting with someone about their career, you could ask, What would you like to learn? Are there committees or teams in our organization on which you would like to participate? What skills are you most proud of? What skills would you like to develop? What gets you most excited to come to work each day? And don't be afraid to ask questions so *you* can improve: *When do you feel most supported at work, and how can I get better at that?*

I also talk about the "feel" that we create for patients and their families when they come into our building. And, you know, that's as simple as eye contact and a smile and, and can I help you? I educate new team members on the Ten and Five rule: When we get ten feet away from someone, make eye contact. When they move closer to five feet, say something. A smile and a simple "good morning" can invite our customers to interact with us.

In terms of positivity, this is where we would discuss the "culture" of your workplace. It's as simple as "how does working here make you *feel?*" And it's that complex. When we did our workplace satisfaction survey after we implemented the principles in this book, we had transformational numbers. Most of our employees would recommend working at KSB to their friends and family.

When you walk into KSB, prepare to feel welcomed. From the person who greets you at the reception desk to the people in the hallways. Our employees make eye contact, they say hello, they are helpful. In fact, I even had someone tell me people were so warm and inviting, the visitor wondered, "Do I know this person?"

You will hear employees say, "Can I help you? Can I help you find where you're going? Did you have any questions about anything?" It's not just business as usual, head down, walk onto your next place, but engaging with people. That is incredibly important in our community. We share our positivity with others.

Develop Outstanding Listening Skills and Practice Them Regularly

There are many books out there on developing listening skills. However, it is an important element of our Supercharged Principle One, so we will touch on it here. More than anything, I think asking great questions has another piece: compassionate listening. Compassionate listening means:

1. You don't jump in and try to "fix it" right away. Allow the other person to speak fully.

2. If it's a complaint or problem, do not get defensive or take it personally.

3. Be patient—too many of us try to finish another person's sentence or "help" them find the right word. (Guess what? That's actually *not* helpful.) For certain personality types (very often us C-Suite folks who have very busy schedules and a long list of responsibilities, and who often have a "time is money" mentality), this is a habit you will have to work at changing.

4. Do not be instantly "reactive." If you don't have an answer, it is perfectly fine to say, "Let me get back to you on that after I look into it." (But then make sure you, indeed, follow up. That is an essential key to developing trust.)

You may have heard of the term "active listening." There are a variety of approaches or concepts, but most of them have some variation of these elements.

1. Pay attention. Eye contact and body language should reflect that you are interested in what the other person is saying, that you are "present." You should *just* be listening and not checking your phone, glancing at your Apple Watch when it pings, or otherwise indicating you are impatient.

2. Be "active" in your listening. This means that yes, you are listening, but with more than just your ears. Observe the other person's body language and facial expressions. For example, we have all asked someone on our team how things are going and they have *said* one thing, but their eyes or anxious

appearance implied something else. You need to actively pay attention to these other nonverbal cues and clues.

3. Be active in *your* unspoken cues. Nod your head. Occasionally add a filler like, "Go on," or some short, encouraging phrase showing you would like the speaker to continue. Ensure you are not presenting with arms folded across your chest or other "closed" body language expressions.

4. "Mirror" or provide feedback. You can use the technique of mirroring in order to ensure you have "heard" the intended message. "What I am hearing you say is . . ." and repeating back, in your own words, what you thought the other person said.

5. Ask open-ended follow-up questions if needed.

6. Respond appropriately. Demonstrate empathy, understanding, and compassion, and withhold judgment. If it is a situation requiring a plan of action, discuss when you will get back to the person and then do so.

Be Accessible and Show an Interest in Member Concerns

As I shared on the first page of this chapter, I am much more accessible than I used to be since I started this journey. I have an open-door policy, and I mean it. But I think about my accessibility, as well, and am proactive about ways to improve it.

To give you an example, I have two emails. One is my first initial and last name. If you, too, have a last name with extra vowels, or one that is mispronounced (Shiner, anyone?), or that

> **Think about your accessibility—and proactive ways to improve it.**

has alternative spellings, or is unusual or originated in a language other than English, some people will misspell it or their emails won't reach you. That does not help me to be accessible.

The solution was pretty darn simple. I have a "David@KSBhospital" email too. Problem solved. More than that—accessibility granted. Your IT team can create this second email address and mirror it to your existing account in about thirty seconds. Do it today!

I finish my presentation at every new employee orientation session by giving them my personal cellphone aside from my office number. I tell them "if six months from now, KSB Hospital is not the best place you've ever worked, please call me." Perhaps you are thinking that sounds like a recipe for getting way too many frivolous calls. Instead, the result has been the opposite.

People seem genuinely touched or appreciative that I trust them enough to give them my personal number as CEO, where they can reach me after hours. After all, though I have my PhD, I am not a medical doctor, who might expect to be "on call" at all hours of the day and night. However, first, it's not an empty gesture. I do mean that if an employee is troubled by something in the workplace, even if it's after hours, I want to hear from them. However, in all the years I have been offering that cellphone number, I have only had three or four calls. Most people instead utilize my accessibility during the workday.

I will be the first to admit that I live and breathe the hospital and the community where I work and where I am a part of the fabric. I realize, for example, a CEO with two thousand employees cannot do what I do (why not?). However, consider your personal standards of accessibility, and how you will listen and interact with your stakeholders.

What can you do to show your people that you are invested in their concerns? (We will cover more of this in the next chapter on engagement.) I tend to respond to emails right away. Sometimes within a few minutes. It's how I stay on top of my inbox and may speak to a bit of my personal obsessiveness with staying on top of my inbox, but it is also important for me to show my stakeholders they are important to me. Perhaps you cannot possibly respond to all your emails in a large company—response time should still reflect your commitment to accessibility, whether that's via an assistant or delegating the email to the proper department.

In terms of accessibility, what does that mean in your company? If someone calls me with an urgent matter and would like to meet with me ASAP, I will attempt to move other appointments around to try to make the accommodation work. But I also know, in healthcare, physicians sometimes don't even have time to eat. So, one person may ask for a meeting and a face-to-face. Others may want to meet me in the hallway for a fast ten-minute discussion. Either of those is fine. It's about what your people need. Meet them where they are.

Find Ways to Express Gratitude

Sometimes a job is transactional. You work. You get a paycheck. Simple. Except for many people (in fact, most), a job is much more. In fact, a BetterUp survey concluded that nine out of ten people would accept earning less money if their work was meaningful to them.[31] This is not to say that you should not pay your team fairly. Every employee in our organization can find on our internal intranet their hourly rate compared to industry and regional benchmarks. However, it is to say that a job is often "more" than "just a job."

---

31   Shawn Achor, Andrew Reece, Gabriella Rosen Kellerman, and Alexi Robichaux, "9 Out of 10 people are willing to earn less money to do more-meaningful work," *Harvard Business Review*, November 6, 2018, accessed May 1, 2023, https://hbr.org/2018/11/9-out-of-10-people-are-willing-to-earn-less-money-to-do-more-meaningful-work.

For some people, their work friends are more like a "family." For others, in industries like healthcare and other front-line workers, education, or nonprofits, they find deeper meaning and contribution through what they do. Still others feel fulfilled because they get to exercise their creativity.

However, regardless of the reasons someone works, we all like to be recognized for our efforts. But gratitude goes even beyond that. *Gratitude is a mindset.*

Let's go back to our active listening. I can demonstrate that I'm listening by expressing gratitude for what I heard. You may recall earlier in the book how I offered an example of Appreciative Inquiry regarding a hospital bill that was not itemized the way the patient's family wanted. Rather than getting defensive, I can express gratitude: "I'm glad you brought this to my attention. I'm grateful to know this because I was unaware the bill didn't have that information you requested on it. I would hate for you to leave our hospital's family over something fixable like this. I am grateful you are giving us a chance."

Gratitude does not necessarily have to be "thank you," either. You may think of gratitude as admiration for someone on your team: "I admire the way you thought about that and your unique perspective. Tell me more."

Gratitude should also involve recognition. At KSB, we started something called Going the Extra Mile (GEM). It's geared toward employee recognition and gratitude. Anyone can be nominated for that "wow" factor in how they do their job or interact with the public. Someone might have gone above and beyond for a patient. For example, an elderly man was having a very hard time with separation from his wife while he was in the hospital, and one of our nurses sat with him until he felt more settled and then checked on him extra, listened, and offered just that bit of extra hand-holding. I received a lovely note from a family member, and this provided the opportunity to recognize the nurse with a GEM award.

A person might be nominated by their supervisor for doing something extra. The fact is from the people who keep our hospital clean, to our dietary team members, to the phlebotomists, to the nurses, to the doctors, to the accounting department—we *all* make KSB a special place to work.

Generally, about ten people will be nominated each month. Two people will be chosen for recognition as the GEM "winners" (though I dislike the word winner, thus suggesting losers in the context of gratitude). But then I will film a video for our website where I talk about some of the others, four or five, and their stories— who nominated them and why. In addition, any person who was nominated receives a handwritten note of thanks from me.

Every corporate culture is unique, so only you will know the best way to express gratitude to your employees for their hard work, so that they "hear" they are appreciated.

Obviously, bonuses and raises demonstrate appreciation. However, here are some other ideas for employee appreciation that you might implement:

1. Gamification. In companies where productivity or deadlines are an issue, offering a rewards program for completing tasks or making an exceptionally difficult target can be a great way to show appreciation. Prizes can be extra days off, or modest gifts or gift cards. For most people, it's the recognition that's meaningful. But a prize is always welcome!

2. Feed them, Part One! One CEO I interviewed during my research said his family of origin celebrates with meals,

so he adopts the same tactic with his work family. We all love a free lunch. Whether it's buying pizza for a team that had to stay late to complete a report, or a team dinner, feeding your employees is a great gesture of goodwill and appreciation. I've learned over the years that it's especially important to recognize those people who work evenings, nights, and weekends. One caveat here. Keep in mind that food is often cultural. Offering a free meal during Ramadan, for example, is disrespectful. Offering pork, when various religions do not allow it, is risky. There should always be options, which should include meatless or vegetarian, or other variety that ensures *everyone* you are feeding feels seen and appreciated.

3. Feed them, Part Two! In addition to departmental lunches and the like, I try to invite groups to have lunch with me—people from all different departments and levels of the hospital, to discuss a specific topic of interest. That one-on-one time is invaluable. It also lets me connect with them—which is what this whole chapter is about—on a deeper level. There's no agenda. No PowerPoint. Just lunch and conversation about a subject they have demonstrated a certain passion about.

4. Recognition awards. Just as with our GEM awards, expressing gratitude can be just that—expressing appreciation for a job well done.

5. Celebrate milestones. Whether it's a pin, a cake, or a bouquet or gift card, celebrating milestones is a terrific way to say "thank you for your loyalty and your dedication." If it has been an extended period of time since you've celebrated, make something up and celebrate away!

6. An annual volunteer day. Increasingly, companies are recognizing that work is great, but employees want that meaning. Offering a paid day off to volunteer is something that is a simple yet effective way to say "thanks."

7. Wellness offerings. Some companies will bring in a yoga teacher and offer classes during lunch hours. Many companies now offer benefits like gym memberships or alternative healthcare as part of their benefits package.

8. Sporting events or other out-of-the-office treats. Who doesn't love a baseball game? Tickets to events are another wonderful way to show your team that you appreciate them. Some companies plan all sorts of off-site events to celebrate the "wins." We took over a hundred people to a minor league baseball game, and they were welcome to bring family members. It was a great way to connect.

Every company will be different, but what is not different is the value of this for morale. According to Work.com, 69 percent of employees will feel and be more productive if they have recognition. A whopping 78 percent say recognition drives their motivation.[32]

However, remember that sincere appreciation and expressions of gratitude, skills you will hone through Supercharged Communications, go a long way. I bet every single person reading this book can recall a time in which someone at work expressed gratitude—not a financial reward, but sincere thanks—and how it made them feel.

---

32   HRCLoud.com, "The importance of employee appreciation for organizational success," May 11, 2022, accessed May 3, 2023, https://www.hrcloud.com/blog/the-importance-of-employee-appreciation-for-organizational-success#:~:text=Employee%20appreciation%20improves%20employee%20performance,recognition%20drives%20their%20motivation%20levels.

 Find Ways to Interact through Rounding

This piece is one I absolutely love as I've implemented it. The idea of rounding came from Quint Studer and has gained tremendous momentum in healthcare. Most of us have watched enough medical drama television to know doctors and nurses "make rounds." As I did my research, I adopted this concept in a nonmedical sense.

No more hiding in the office. Rounding is exactly what it sounds like—making rounds. In my case, I walk the hospital (and I also visit our satellite clinics, which entails driving to them off-site). You might walk the factory floor, or through various departments. In a large company, you would obviously break it up, perhaps trying to get to each department once or twice a year, or once a quarter. But it's important to be seen—this is about connecting. No more hiding in the office. I round in each department or clinic every quarter.

It was actually my wife who helped me to understand how important rounding is. When I was first named CEO, I understandably immersed myself in "the weeds" of it. The board of directors saw me. I went to a *lot* of meetings. But I wasn't out and about in the hospital. An employee engagement survey we did revealed that people didn't think they saw me enough. I had very little visibility—except to the board and department heads. I asked my wife, a nurse, about my approach to the hospital. She was frank: did I want the truth—or did I want her to tell me how great I was? While I wouldn't have minded the latter, I told her to be honest.

She said I was not visible enough—the survey was true. Being seen, outside of meetings, for a few minutes a day was not enough of a presence—and it wasn't doing anything for my employee engagement.

I started doing rounds. At first, I sprinted through the hospital. I smiled and waved—think of it as a fly-by. I could cover the whole place in ten minutes. Bad idea. That was not enough, but I was new to it and starting to find my way. As I have evolved in my rounding, I knew I needed to make more time. Every leader faces this sort of challenge.

For me, I started cutting my meetings—ten minutes here, twenty minutes there. I instructed my administrative assistant to make sixty-minute meetings fifty minutes and thirty-minute meetings twenty-five minutes. I was amazed at the positive impact this small change made in my day. I also took a hard look at whether I even needed to be *at* some of them. I think, depending on your leadership position, sometimes you are invited because teams think they "should" invite you. But many times, I might only need to be there for the first ten minutes—or not at all. Not only did I and my assistant clean up my schedule so I could do proper rounding, but when employees had access to me—on my rounds, in the hallways, visiting their clinics—we had impromptu conversations, or I learned what I needed to by being *there,* so my presence in a chair in a conference room was not necessary.

By the way, since I fell into that trap myself, I now feel *always* being in meetings is fundamentally wrong in any business. I think it's harmful for the stock price. I think it's harmful for productivity. I think it's harmful for retention. I think as an executive, and especially as a CEO or president or owner, you have to build time in your schedule to make this happen. Because if you don't schedule room for it, it's not going to happen. You also need to make clear to those around you that this cannot be the thing that your assistant always schedules over when they need extra hours because they always will. You will have direct reports that are critical of you being in their space. Too bad. Rounding is too important to listen to the detractors. Invite them to come along with you.

During my rounds, I see as many people as I can. Sometimes it's extremely casual—dropping by a nurses' station to ask how things are going, stopping to chat with someone from housekeeping, or spending a few minutes with a doctor catching up.

Other times, I have a little more of a focus. Often, while I'm on a floor or wing of the hospital or at a clinic, I will try to walk with my chief of staff or the department director. I always end with, "Is there anything that I can do for you?" I will offer a general thank you to the department or a group of employees if we have had a discussion. In addition, I make sure the department head gives me positive news— someone I should recognize for a new idea for streamlining a process, or someone's birthday, or whatever it is. This deepens the encounters.

In healthcare, but truly in every company, there are often crises. I could be rounding, and the person I planned to talk to could be in the middle of something. That's fine. In fact, that's great. Because what rounding should NOT be is a photo-op-type situation, where everything is picture-perfect, and everyone's trying to impress the CEO. That's not the purpose, and we need to make sure we keep that top of mind. The purpose is about *them*. It is about being the best part of *their* day—their real, imperfect, occasionally messy, and in-crisis day. Sometimes we find small suggestions we can immediately take action to correct. That's a huge win!

When I go up to the ICU, I can tell if there's someone who has the capacity to talk for a few minutes about something. The more you do rounding in your organization, the better you will get at that discernment. I also understand that if they've got a full unit, they do not have that capacity. Then I say good morning—and that's it. I don't try to slow them down, get in their way, or make them feel as if they "must" stop what they are doing because the CEO is there. However, if I see a person who's maybe sitting at their workstation and they engage with me, then I generally let them go on for as long as they want to go, in most cases, and I let them drive that. Access is my mission.

One example I heard from my research is one of the CEOs who did this form of rounding had his chief nursing officer give him a note that morning before they rounded to say things like: "ER's too busy, we're not going to go down there today."

That kind of heads-up is really important from the people who have the pulse of the department. For example, someone at our hospital came up with an idea about how to do stickers on our charts differently. It saved us a few pennies a sheet—but over an entire hospital, day in and day out, that added up to real savings. I was able, in real time, essentially, to walk into that department and say to that person, "I heard about what you did with the stickers. That's amazing, and here is the impact your idea will make on our organization!"

 ## Start with Yes

I added this element to this chapter because this is where it fits—in engagement and connection. I try to encourage everyone at KSB to "start with yes."

We are an entity that deals with people. But we're not selling socks. We are on the front lines of interactions at critical moments in people's lives. In addition, as a team, we're all in the business of saving lives and making lives better. I encourage us all to start with the positive. If it's possible and within your power to do so, start with yes and make it happen. For supervisors and leaders, I ask them to remain open—to start with yes. When a suggestion is made by an employee, for example, the response cannot be, "We've always done it that way," or "We tried that in 1987 and it didn't work." Or a fast no with no listening. If you immediately shut down, or say no, or I can't help you—then the conversation's over. The chance for engagement has evaporated.

A "yes, and . . ." is so much better than a "no, but . . ."

Recap . . . and What's Next

I hope this chapter has started you thinking of ways you can increase engagement in your own organization. Our principles in this chapter included:

1. Ask great questions and generate positivity.

2. Develop outstanding listening skills and practice them regularly.

3. Be accessible and show an interest in member concerns.

4. Find ways to express gratitude.

5. Find ways to interact through rounding.

We covered how to actively listen, as well as why expressing gratitude is so important to your team—and ways to do so.

Finally, we discussed the concept of "rounding" and accessibility. You don't have to be in the medical field to make rounds. You merely need to be visible and interact with the people in your company in order to demonstrate your personal commitment to Supercharged Communication and engagement.

Now, we'll move on more deeply into engagement. This next chapter will get into the details of the various mediums through which you can connect with your stakeholders.

*The single biggest problem in communication
is the illusion that it has taken place.*

—GEORGE BERNARD SHAW

SUPERCHARGED PRINCIPLE TWO

Engage with Intent through Various Mediums

Text, Slack, apps, emails, voicemails, vlogs, blogs, social media channels . . . we have more ways to connect with our stakeholders than ever before. Yet, as the famous line goes from *Cool Hand Luke,* "What we've got here is a failure to communicate."

It seems, despite all the tools at our disposal, sometimes we're still playing the old children's game of "telephone," where messaging gets distorted. Or, we are so bombarded with communication that after a while we just shut out all the noise.

In addition, our business communications have bled into our personal lives, blurring work–life balance. And the global COVID-19 pandemic only made these problems worse.

In this chapter, we're going to talk about engaging with *intent,* and doing so through various *mediums.* Our second Supercharged Communication Principle has five elements:

Engage with intent through various medium.

Find a rhythm of regular communication with key constituents.

Be transparent with high frequency.

Use multiple channels to communicate your message.

Look for ways to overcome engagement challenges.

In times of crisis be intentional about communicating differently.

Let's explore how to reach our stakeholders with the best methodology.

Find a Rhythm of Regular Communication with Key Constituents

Every organization and leader is different, but we all must find the best way to reach our constituents, as well as the rhythm (how often).

I'll share with you a story about my first communication rhythms when I got excited and developed my concepts on Supercharged Communications. At first, I thought, "I can't overdo the communications." What that ended up looking like though was *bombardment*. I had newsletters. Emails. Vlogs. Updates via text. You name it, and I was sending it!

I thought my videos were especially great. I also thought they should be about five to ten minutes, and I was sending them pretty much daily. They were posted on our website.

My first clue that I was overdoing it should have been . . . I was running out of things to say.

And *sometimes,* super-important stuff was embedded in those videos—along with other lighter things. But it took an encounter with an employee to enlighten me. I was chatting with a nurse, and she asked me a question that I had posted in a video. When I mentioned that to her, she said, "Oh . . . those? No offense, but I don't have *time* to look at those. I never watch them."

After I scraped my ego off the floor, I gave it a long, hard examination. I realized a couple of things:

1. We are all very busy.

2. While some people may appreciate constant updates, others are "bottom line" folks and just want to know what they *need* to know.

3. If employees (especially in a busy hospital) have no time to view or read through lengthy updates at work, you are encroaching onto their precious personal time and are infringing on their work–life balance by thinking they will then view or read these things at home.

For me, I had to look at *all* my communication and examine the effectiveness of each medium as well as its frequency. I will discuss this more in the section on multiple channels. Eventually, I found what worked for me and my organization. Most of my videos and communications are now weekly. And some I play by ear. And every video has a running transcription. An employee made this suggestion, and I implemented it that day.

In terms of frequency, too, I wanted to share a story that occurred during the COVID-19 pandemic. I am going to share part of it here and part in the very next section.

Every single aspect of our lives was impacted by the pandemic crisis. However, as front-line workers at a hospital, our experiences were especially difficult. Our employees were very understandably rattled, overworked, stressed—and rightfully terrified they would bring this awful virus home to their own families.

In addition, since this was a novel coronavirus, the scientific community was learning about it in real time. Some of its ravages were not like anything the medical community had seen before—even as compared to a bad flu. Lungs were left with holes and organs failed in some patients, and deterioration was often swift. It acted in brutal ways—and how to treat it, exactly, was still unknown. It was highly contagious. It killed people indiscriminately. Add to that, the sheer volume of patients and the scale of the crisis left most hospitals with critical shortages of essential needs like personal protective equipment (PPE). In addition, staff was getting sick as well, causing personnel shortages. And the fact that this was *global* was a factor. This meant that it wasn't as if New York City was in crisis, but Los Angeles wasn't—so nursing support, equipment, etc., could not be shared one to the other. Everyone was in crisis.

As the CEO of the hospital, I felt the need to communicate *daily*. Sometimes twice a day. I was trying to pass on any grain of information I had. While this may sound like a very proactive and logical approach to the crisis, in retrospect it actually did not help us. Now I will explain why.

Be Transparent with High Frequency

This was an area I had to learn and take to heart as I gathered all my data.

As a leader, but specifically a leader in a rural area, I have known some of the people I work with for decades. We employ a significant percentage of the people of Dixon (we are the first- or second-largest employer). And if we don't employ residents directly, then the companies where they work may support us. That can include car dealerships, restaurants, hotels, and pretty much any business that counts on the business of the hospital or its visitors and employees. We are vital to the economic health of our community.

In addition, as a smaller town/rural area, employees have families. So, if we employ someone, we also then impact their families and friends, further deepening our bonds with the community. Basically, and I mean this sincerely, if you live in Dixon, it is impossible *not* to know someone who either works at the hospital or has a family member who does.

While this might give you the warm fuzzies, what it meant for me personally was that I always had a paternal instinct of "Don't tell people about troubles and don't make them worry."

That was just wrong.

When it's appropriate, I have learned to pass along the bad news, to be transparent, whether that is a financial issue (and I do not know of a hospital that isn't under pressure because of our dysfunctional reimbursement methods, the aftereffects of COVID, and so on) or something else. I don't pass along information that is a "rumor" or that I do not yet know for sure. But our hospital impacts our employees' lives, and they deserve to know what is going on.

I told you I would finish my pandemic story here. I was communicating daily—every crumb of information. I had by now committed to transparency and was curbing my paternal instincts. However, as you may recall from the pandemic, information was changing, sometimes minute to minute.

This virus was behaving in both expected and unexpected ways. The evening news was leading with death tolls and video clips of city hospitals that were overrun with patients and running out of beds and ventilators; in some large cities, they required refrigerator trucks for all of the bodies. It was horrifying. Mental health issues multiplied.

Parents struggled with child care issues as schools were closed. As life has returned to near-new normal at the time of this writing, it can be easy to dismiss it all as a bad dream (except for those millions whose lives and families' lives were shattered by death and serious illness/long COVID). However, at the time, we were all desperate to know what to do and how to keep ourselves and our loved ones safe. Consequently, I was trying to pass along every scrap of information.

In addition, while I do not wish to get into politics, in our organization we follow the science. At the beginning of the pandemic, I stated to our board of directors and leadership team that, regardless of political views, KSB Hospital would be acting based on guidance from trusted resources and regulatory bodies. We had people upset by what I was passing along. As the Centers for Disease Control and Prevention (CDC), World Health Organization (WHO), the National Institutes of Health (NIH), and Illinois Department of Public Health learned about the virus, analyzed the science, and provided updated guidance, for some people that changing guidance caused upset and a lack of trust. In crises, I totally understand that emotional reaction.

The fact that I was passing along information daily (even when nothing had changed) opened up everything I said to scrutiny. Ultimately, I opted to remain transparent but cut down on update after update. My mindset and approach was "We're going to follow the science." However, I stopped updates when there was no changing news. I also waited until we had clear guidance before passing along information.

Now, transparency is not just a "crisis communication" strategy. Leading with transparency is essential in other areas and for a variety of reasons:

1. Your decisions do not just impact your organization. They impact real lives. Those real lives are attached to other people as well—families, friends, etc., of your employees. Life

decisions are made based on information you share—and you owe it to your stakeholders to be clear. People move for jobs, they purchase homes based on their jobs, their partners make decisions based on their loved one's position. That responsibility for transparency should not be taken lightly.

2. Transparency also applies to expectations. I am sure every reader has had an experience, or knows a colleague or friend who has, of working for that "impossible boss"—the one who was never satisfied, but also never made *clear* what his or her expectations are. Clear expectations enable employees to thrive. When you know what is expected, you can create processes to achieve that.

3. Transparency—even about troubles—is healthier than the alternative. So much anxiety can revolve around layoffs, mergers and acquisitions, and other corporate decisions that impact employees but that they have no control over. Lack of control, in any situation, exacerbates anxiety. It also makes the workplace ripe for gossip. Understandably, there are often negotiations or discussions happening in the boardroom that must be kept confidential. However, be transparent enough to say, "Yes, we're in trouble and in the red, and we're working to find solutions," or "Yes, the company is for sale. As soon as we have information we can share, we will provide it." Hopefully through the techniques in this book, you have been developing deeper trust through Supercharged Communications—and if that is the case, then offering a truthful, "I am not sure but I promise to tell you when I am sure," will be taken at face value and appreciated.

4. You may have heard the saying (about passing along information): "Is it true? Is it kind? Is it helpful?" This is often said regarding

gossip or imparting criticism. However, I think it holds true in the corporate world too. You might think of it this way: "Is it true— and shareable (i.e., not confidential)? Is it being presented in the most compassionate and transparent way possible? Is it helpful, useful—or necessary—to this team or individual?"

Next, we'll discuss the channels of communication.

 Use Multiple Channels to Communicate Your Message

Think about how you personally "run your life." Google calendar? Outlook? A family whiteboard in the kitchen? All of the above? How do you get your "news"? Watching a specific news show or shows every day? Scrolling through a news site? Twitter or a crowd-sourced site? How is your inbox? If your supervisor had to get in touch with you and sent an email, do you even have time to check it in a timely fashion? What about texts?

Once upon a time, communication was fairly straightforward. The number of television channels was limited. Corporate communications involved newspapers, the evening news, a press release, a company newsletter, and, later, email became integral. That is not the case today.

What I have discovered in my Supercharged Communications research is you need to use multiple channels. You need to meet your people and stakeholders where they are.

Let's look at seven main channels of communication.

1. Face-to-face (I include Zoom in here since the pandemic.)

2. TV, radio, and broadcast communications

3. Mobile communications, including texts

4. Phone messages, voicemails

5. Slack and other instant messaging channels and internal communication channels/intranets

6. Email

7. Social media

Every organization has internal communications and external communications. For the purposes of this book, I am focusing more on the Supercharged Communications internally. However, of course, many of these principles apply to communicating with people outside your organization and external stakeholders.

First, consider that different channels are best suited for certain messaging or tasks. Let's take a company in an area where there are hurricanes or blizzards. Texts and automated voicemails to let employees know the offices are closed are more effective than trying to reach them on Slack or social media, or even email (unless your company makes clear that emails from HR will be the notification method).

Certainly, no one should learn they are being laid off via a tweet. Twitter, now X, is part of a communications strategy—but corporate communications have many channels. Social apps generally are not ideal for complex crises, for example, because of the limits of word count and a necessity for extreme conciseness.

More involved information (items with a lot of moving parts; legal responses; communications with numbers, statistics, and detailed analyses, etc.) is often better via email or on your website, so people can refer to it.

And there are some things that simply need to be done face-to-face, whether that is in small groups or with leadership on stage.

Combining communication methods is the most effective. This is an *inclusive* approach. As I have written, you need to reach people where they are. By where they are—particularly today with scattered departments across the globe, telework, hybrid work, and so on—it means they can access it where they need to (on their phone, on an app, on their computer). However, it also means where they are in a more philosophical sense.

Just as the nurse told me she had no time to access my many (too many) videos, we all have different approaches to tech and how we use it and receive it. For example, millennials tend to prefer text to phone calls. In fact, a study in Europe showed that using a phone as an actual phone (to make calls) was only the fifth most common use over other apps.[33] Millennials also tend to prefer the immediacy of text over email, for example.[34] Be mindful that certain jobs do not have access to computers while at work. For example, our housekeeping team members don't have computers. On the flip side, Boomers or older workers may not like utilizing text or Slack as a main way to communicate in the workplace.

Meeting people where they are, including in their attitudes toward tech and communications, means utilizing a mix of channels and messaging.

Look for Ways to Overcome Engagement Challenges

"Engagement" has a lot of buzzy noise about it. We are told, as leaders, that employee engagement is essential. In fact, according to a *Harvard Business Review* survey, 92 percent of executives feel that engaged employees perform better.[35]

---

33   Larry Alton, "How do millennials prefer to communicate?" May 11, 2017, accessed June 1, 2023, https://www.forbes.com/sites/larryalton/2017/05/11/how-do-millennials-prefer-to-communicate/?sh=32d532346d6f.

34   Ibid.

35   Pulse Survey, "A winning approach to employee success," *Harvard Business Review*, July 5, 2020, accessed May 23, 2023, https://www.quantumworkplace.com/winning-approach-to-employee-success.

But what does *engagement* actually mean?

Employee engagement is the connection an employee feels, both emotionally and mentally, to their team and their workplace/organization, as well as the work they do. Engaged employees demonstrate enthusiasm. They also are more productive and willing to go that extra mile (like our GEM candidates that I discussed earlier).

Engagement is not a one-size-fits-all situation. And there are always barriers to successful engagement.

One such barrier is lack of a clear mission (which is what we will cover in our next chapter). When teams and employees don't know the mission, then there can be lack of focus on the part of employees. At our board meetings, our mission is referred to time and time again. We remain committed to our ideals, and I sincerely believe that KSB has that "secret sauce" of engagement—and that clarity is a part of why it's a great place to work.

> **Engaged employees demonstrate enthusiasm. They also are more productive and willing to go that extra mile**

In fact, recently, one of our doctors was accepted to an exclusive program specifically meant to address physician wellness. She found among her peers that the largest factor contributing to physician burnout was hospital leadership and administration. These doctors felt unheard and unappreciated—by the very people they should be working closely with.

Upon her return she said, "Thankfully we don't have that problem at our hospital." We take our commitment to our people very seriously, and we align our mission from the top down and bottom up.

Another common engagement issue is information overload or saturation. Some of this may stem from processes that are not streamlined—so repetitive information is sent . . . and sent again. Once again, technology, which was supposed to help us communicate better, can be the barrier. For example, companies can have dozens or even hundreds of different types of technology (everything from customer relationship management [CRM] tools to data entry to intranet and more). When employees feel overloaded, it all becomes just so much noise. Thus, your communications plans should be well-thought-out in terms of what you are trying to accomplish, and they should be as streamlined as possible. I brought in an outside consulting team to visit departments and ask questions about the how and when of our messaging. Based on what they discovered, we created a three-minute message that goes out every Wednesday. We were told we have too many places to look and employees don't have time to follow all the various sites. "Give me one place to look," so we did just that with the Three-Minute Message!

A Day in the Life: Kirk Stewart, MD, 3rd-Year Family Medicine Resident

Advanced Strangulation Training Supports Vital Care for Trauma Patients

KSB Center for Wound Healing Receives Excellence in Clinical Distinction and Patient Satisfaction Awards

Krista Hobbs Selected as First Getting the Extra Margin (GEM) Winner

Another barrier to engagement is inconsistent communications. While in crisis this may change, communications—regardless of your medium—should be consistent. If you send out a monthly newsletter, skipping a month here or there or consistently putting it out late will mean employees stop looking for it. They cannot count on it, so it becomes an afterthought.

Engagement is something that is palpable. I wrote about our GEM awards. We love hearing from patients and their families who contact us and say, "I can't believe this person did this." We talk about the miracles happening at KSB every day, because every day we have that happen. You don't teach that. You hire the right people, and they do amazing things because they are awesome people good at their jobs and engaged with our mission to serve our community.

In Times of Crisis Be Intentional about Communicating Differently

As I shared, the global COVID-19 pandemic created crises in nearly every area of our lives from supply chain to access to healthcare (e.g., elective surgeries at all or most hospitals were halted in an "all-hands-on-deck" approach to the vast numbers of sick people showing up in the emergency room).

However, there are other types of crises. Every day, corporations face crisis events, including:

1. Financial crises. Our hospital is one of many that have faced this as the pandemic raged and created other problems for hospitals aside from so many people falling sick; costs of operations and personnel shot up. We have all seen headlines of bankruptcies in corporate America, events like the fall of Enron, or when the auto industry was rescued as "too big to fail." Recently, there was the Silicon Valley Bank failure. In my sector, 194 rural hospitals have closed since January 2005.[36]

2. Organizational crises. These crises might be malfeasance or other scandals related to leadership, or other headline-making disasters, often when a company's bad behavior comes to light. Sometimes this will involve whistleblowers exposing

---

36   UNC; Rural Hospital Closures—Sheps Center (unc.edu), accessed June 10, 2023.

organizational failures—such as suppressing something dangerous in one of their products.

3. Personnel crises. We saw this firsthand during the pandemic. Many businesses had to shutter because they simply could not find people to fill positions. Parents were pressed thin by having to supervise school-age children (including their online education) with a lack of daycare/school. Another form of personnel crises occurs when someone who is the "face" or voice of a company makes a huge mistake—such as a decade ago when the CEO of Lululemon body-shamed their customers. Bad behaviors, such as sexual harassment, "hot mic" moments exposing cruelty or arrogance, unpopular opinions, and so on are all personnel crises.

4. Natural disasters. Obviously, the COVID-19 pandemic was a worldwide disaster. Global companies deal with global disasters often. Hurricanes, tornadoes, earthquakes, wildfires— it seems as if our planet is on fire, and this is creating crises for businesses. Crisis information and communications include the care and well-being of your employees and getting them safety information and updates. In addition, unprepared companies can end up with a PR disaster on their hands, not just a natural one. Or worse! You may recall that employees at a candle factory were killed when a tornado swept through in December of 2021. However, in the aftermath, employees claimed they were threatened to be fired if they did not stay on the job—despite a tornado warning being in effect.[37]

---

37   Meredith Deliso, "Employees of Kentucky candle factory destroyed by deadly tornado file new lawsuit," December 9, 2022, accessed May 10, 2023, https://abcnews. go.com/US/employees-kentucky-candle-factory-destroyed-deadly-tornado-file/ story?id=94868226.

5. Tech Crises. Data breaches and data privacy concerns, system and social media crashes, hacking incidents, and the like present a challenge and their own type of crisis. Technological crises can impact the bottom line (e.g., lost sales, leads, or customer data). However, they can also cause great reputational damage.

The pandemic caught the whole globe off-guard. However, every large business or hospital will face a crisis at some point. Therefore, you should have a crisis communications plan.

In crisis, it is important for nonessential communication to decrease for a time. Laser focus needs to be on the matter at hand. In order to communicate effectively in times of crisis, first, as a leader, you must identify your key messaging.

What is the most important thing(s) your employees and stake-holders need to know? During the pandemic, in a hospital, advising on safety protocols was at the top of the list. Keeping it simple and focused is best. Your key messaging should summarize the crisis (briefly), address both business and employee-related issues—but also be "human." A crisis communication during a natural disaster, for instance, should reflect concern for the human toll. If a CEO is removed from the company for something like sexual harassment, acknowledging that toxicity and the victims is appropriate.

Your crisis communications plan should also be intentional about the channels and mediums you will be utilizing. So, for example, we all know during a weather-related crisis we can turn on certain television channels and see FEMA giving us information, including with sign language interpreters and a "crawl" on the bottom of the screen. We can count on that. If during a particular crisis you decide email (because it carries a greater degree of professionalism in many people's opinion) is your main medium, along with website updates, let your employees know that. By doing so, you do not add to their anxiety with them wondering "Will I get a text? When will we have an update?" Don't make your employees guess where to find critical information. Tell them where to look!

Do not forget your social media communications, as well. Because of the immediacy of the internet, getting "ahead" of a crisis will usually require communicating through the social channels your corporation utilizes.

In terms of communication style, social will have a different "voice" than a formal email sent to all employees. There are brands and companies that are masterful social communicators. A great example is the hamburger chain Wendy's, which uses humor expertly. By connecting with their customers, they have built trust and real social media fans, which would no doubt help them if a crisis arises.

Intention must also include transparency. The best example of that is Johnson & Johnson. In fact, they are literally studied as a "textbook case" of how to handle crisis communications. In 1982, a 'til-this-day-unknown person or persons laced Tylenol capsules with cyanide. J&J stopped all other communications and through a massive undertaking, communicated to hundreds of thousands of healthcare providers to tell their patients not to take Tylenol. (This was before the internet exploded, so it truly was an enormous task.) This tragic crisis was *not* J&J's fault. Yet they were transparent about it and went on to create tamper-proof packaging (so if you ever feel like opening packaging is like breaking into Fort Knox, this is one of the events that initiated that). Consumers did not reject Tylenol or J&J—their transparency helped make them a trusted brand for over-the-counter pain relievers to this day.

Perhaps most importantly, immediacy is essential in times of crisis. When your employees and stakeholders are not informed, it creates an information vacuum. When there is a vacuum, gossip, false information, rumors, and even outright hostility can take its place. I often remind our administrative team, in the absence of information, people make shit up.

In Supercharged Communications, you must lead with intention.

 ## A Story of Engagement

I wanted to share a story from my research that I think perfectly illustrates engaging with your stakeholders in a variety of mediums. A mid-sized public hospital needed a new building in order to be able to serve their community. Their board members were elected by the community. Everyone knew that this was desperately needed. However, elected hospital board members and many people in the community were insistent that there could be no new taxes to pay for it.

The CEO's response was to engage with the community—her stakeholders. She was intentional—and she thought outside the box. Her approach was, "I'm going to go everywhere I possibly can." Whether it was the Rotary Club, or Chamber of Commerce meetings, luncheons or events, she was willing to speak and welcomed the opportunity.

However, she had the brilliant idea to have a mock patient room built and allow the public to come in and walk through it. Seeing it in three dimensions, where people could touch and admire the technology and the cheerful rooms, helped to make the idea of the new hospital "real." They were able to see the vision. The elected board members switched over their votes to a yes, and eventually, the referendum to build the new hospital passed.

This was because their CEO said, "I am going to create a picture of what this is going to look like." She engaged with her stakeholders in a clever, powerful way. Using Appreciative Inquiry concepts, she encouraged the community to dream, and it worked!

Recap . . . and a Look Ahead

Here in Supercharged Principle Two, we focused on communications. We have five essential concepts:

1. Find a rhythm of regular communication with key constituents.

2. Be transparent with high frequency.

3. Use multiple channels to communicate your message.

4. Look for ways to overcome engagement challenges.

5. In times of crisis be intentional about communicating differently.

Communications, we discussed, is not a "one-size-fits-all" topic. What is right for a rural hospital in Illinois might not be the right approach for a hospital in a major city—or a global corporation. However, the principle works for all. Establishing how often you communicate with your stakeholders for the most impact, across the best channels, is essential—as is transparency.

Communications is also a key ingredient in engagement—it supercharges the trust between you and your stakeholders.

Now, we will examine our mission—and how to present a united leadership team.

Management must speak with one voice.
When it doesn't management itself becomes a
peripheral opponent to the team's mission.

—PAT RILEY

SUPERCHARGED PRINCIPLE THREE

| *Be Mission-Focused and Present United Leadership* |

You are probably familiar with the "divide and conquer" strategy kids use (whether you have kids—or were once one yourself!). One parent says no, so the child does an end run, asks the other parent and tries to get past the "no." Once kids do that a time or two, parents generally wise up (mine sure did). They learn that presenting a united front is the best defense to those childhood schemes.

In general, leadership—whether parents or a board of directors or a C-Suite—must offer that united front and lead from that strength. A united front builds trust—whether it's a child who learns boundaries and that they can count on their parents to keep them safe and set expectations, or colleagues and teams who feel confident that leadership has a shared vision and is steering the ship.

That trust deepens when leadership has a clear-eyed focus on the bigger mission. The big question is: what is that mission?

Too many of us have become cynical as we see companies and organizations with grand mission statements that sound really good, but then they are not lived. Missions need to be your compass. Bill George coined the term "True North" in his 2007 best-selling book on discovering your authentic leadership style. Your mission clarifies the path through any forest even at times when you can't see it for the trees. So, in this chapter, we will discuss our last Supercharged Communication Principle and the five essential parts to it:

Be mission-focused through united leadership.

Keep the focus on your mission and know your audience—be prepared.

Vocally support team members and encourage healthy debate.

Ensure team members feel informed and included.

Build a structure to support key leaders.

The Executive is part of the community— get involved.

This might be a good time to pull out your Leadership Tree and remind yourself of your vision for how you want to lead. That tree should be a foundational piece of building your personal and professional development plan. It can also help you clarify your own mission.

Keep the Focus on Your Mission and Know Your Audience—Be Prepared

As the CEO of a hospital, if I ever wonder what our mission is, I need only walk the hallways. As part of the fabric of a rural community, if I ever wonder what our mission is, I need only drive through town.

Every corporation or organization has its own unique mission. Companies need to sell products and services, they must answer to their shareholders, or their stakeholders, or the people whom they serve, but aside from that, most companies also have a bigger mission, one that often reflects a commitment to environmental, social, and governance, commonly referred to as ESG. Missions can even include those "big, hairy, audacious goals" (BHAG goals). I would always rather "reach" than settle.

Missions are usually also straightforward—the better to remember it. For example, TED's mission is "Spread ideas." LinkedIn's is "To connect the world's professionals to make them more productive and successful." PayPal's definitely includes a BHAG in it: To build the web's most convenient, secure, cost-effective payment solution. Think of it—the best payment solution on all of the entire web. Pretty audacious!

At our hospital, we also have a concise mission that guides us in all we do. It's our compass when we have to make tough decisions and our compass for how we treat our patients and community.

The mission of Katherine Shaw Bethea Hospital is to restore, maintain, and enhance health by providing superior care now and in the future.

But a mission must be part of your culture if you are to succeed in your lofty goals. If you went into our boardroom, we have our mission on the wall in our boardroom, as many places probably do. The members of the C-Suite around our shiny boardroom table frequently point to it and ask the important question: "The work that we're doing right now, how would we answer this issue or question at hand—are we doing it in the context of our mission?"

We have all seen implosions of companies that have lost sight of their mission, whether that is through unethical practices or lack of innovation. For example, "innovation" is in Dell's mission statement. Initially, they were very innovative. While competitors were only selling in Big Box stores, Dell was selling over the internet. However, Dell missed the boat in the last ten years in terms of innovation, and they failed to keep up with the mobile revolution; now they are playing catch-up.

This guides the entire hospital, as well as our board. For example, if we are considering a big purchase of hospital equipment, it goes back to "does this help us to provide superior care now and in the future?" If you are a "bottom line" kind of person, the mission helps you move past the noise to *the* most important thing.

In a hospital or healthcare setting, patient care is always going to be top of mind—our mission is clear. Whatever your corporate mission, your decisions will be clarified by having a clear mission. I have a saying I go to often when making important decisions that impact our ability to deliver on our mission. We make decisions in this order:

1. Patient First

2. Employee Second

3. Organization Third

I like to think I also have a personal mission—and I think all leaders should. That's why I suggested taking out your tree and giving it another look. I would add I am really committed to spreading the word about Supercharged Communications and Appreciative Inquiry. For instance, I've started teaching a class on Appreciative Inquiry—with the people in the class (all of them volunteered to take it) going out into our hospital—and the world—and creating their own spin on the approach.

Being mission-focused is more than words—it is an amazing decision-making device as well. For example, one of the expressions I live by is: "Be tough-minded on standards but tender-hearted on people." Thus, if there is an incident where our standards lagged, or a mistake occurred, we cannot stand for that, but it is not to come down like a hammer on the person or people who made the error. Instead, with that guidance, our method at KSB would be to start with the mistake, moving backward through every single part of the chain of events, and figure out how we can prevent that error from happening again, delivering the best standards of care. We use an approach called "just culture." Be critical of the process, not the person.

In terms of Supercharged Communications, knowing your mission also helps you distill messaging—does your message reflect your commitment to the mission? In addition, you need to keep in mind your audience—and be prepared. When thinking of your audience, it helps to ask this question (in the Appreciative Inquiry way): If an audience member left the presentation and went out and described the message as one that would exceed my wildest dream, what would she tell her friend?

"Audience" can give the false impression that I am talking about standing on a stage in an auditorium speaking to a large group. An audience can be just one or two people. Regardless, my conversation or messaging with a physician or group of physicians will likely be different from my communications with the head of housekeeping. They have different purposes for meeting with me, and each is equally important. Regardless, I need to adapt to my audience to the issue at hand.

Part of the preparation is the Appreciative Inquiry question I just posed. How am I going to convey my top-of-mind message to this particular person or audience? You can probably see why this is the third principle—it builds on the other two. As we covered in the last chapter, communications should meet people where they are in the mediums and channels that work for them. Tailoring those communications to those channels is essential for successful communications. Knowing my audience helps me choose the right channels, the right message, and the right medium.

A Story about a United Leadership Team

Before we move on, I wanted to share a little story about my leadership team. As I have stated before, when the global pandemic tore through the world, our hospital, like many, experienced its most challenging financial pressures since its origin over 125 years ago.

If you are not in healthcare, you may not realize that much of a hospital's income is derived from its elective surgeries, as well as services like outpatient MRIs, etc. Like most if not all hospitals worldwide, we stopped that part of our operations so we could focus on the crisis at hand. Local, state, and regional authorities forced us to discontinue elective procedures due to the pandemic. We didn't want anyone who didn't *have* to be there coming into the hospital; visitors were no longer allowed. We didn't want visitors getting sick with COVID—or patients catching COVID from visitors. The hospital focused on essential services to emergency patients and the influx of COVID victims.

We also, as a nonprofit hospital, treat the breadth of our community. We even treat prisoners from a nearby prison if emergencies arise or an inmate needs surgery. We have Medicaid patients—and those reimbursements do not even come close to paying for treatment. Hence, again, these other paying services are necessary for our financial health.

When our troubles became obvious, our entire executive team, our physicians, and I all volunteered to take a 10 percent reduction in compensation. We presented a united front on this matter. This is not to say everyone was happy about it—that was a not-insignificant cut. However, when we focused on our *mission,* the need for this decision was clear.

It also sent a message—to everyone at our hospital—that we were willing to make sacrifices in these unprecedented times for the good of our beloved KSB. Sometimes your Supercharged Communications are actions that mirror and align with your principles.

Being united in our mission also means our team holds each other accountable. In fact, we help one another when we hold others accountable. I used to, because of my nature, let things slide. I genuinely care about everyone in our hospital, and I tended to let little things go (and the occasional medium-sized thing too!). However, we weren't getting to where we needed to get to as an organization on our KPIs, and people weren't getting to where they needed to get to as a professional. So that accountability is really important. We begin with board-driven organizational goals that align with our mission. Then we cascade those down into the organization.

Vocally Support Team Members and Encourage Healthy Debate

The principles in this book are put into action each and every day at KSB Hospital. The concept of being tender-hearted with people is put into action every day. We support each other; across all the many departments, there is a warmth that you can see and feel in how people interact with one another.

It's the people is not some empty motto.

Someone asked me recently how we handle the difficult personnel issues, for example, if someone needs to be written up for some kind of behavior or work issue. Again, Supercharged Communications dictate that we would use Appreciative Inquiry. The line of questioning would thus not begin with something like "Do you know why you're being written up?" Instead, we take it back to *before* the incident.

"What would have been a better way to handle this? And let's walk it backward—when were things working perfectly? *Just before* the incident, can you think of any triggers? And then how can we take that information and come up with a plan so next time everything can go better right from start to finish?"

The other piece of this concept is "healthy debate" and this circles back to that idea of accountability. Our board of directors and our leadership team is not a table of "Yes Men" and "Yes Women." Their job is to push me and the hospital to be our very best. We are also very different—our board members come from all different careers. Our hospital leadership—from our chief people officer to our chief nursing officer to our chief of staff and so on—also strive to debate in healthy ways and for us to solve our differences in a manner befitting the values we hold dear. Ideally, we come through the debate with a united solution and plan.

This is not to say we don't have issues. But I encourage us to work through them. For example, last year, in an emergency, someone was sent to x-ray from the ER in a gown on top, jeans still on. It turned out that this particular patient had a weapon (a knife). Not only was this dangerous, it was very late at night when there was only one x-ray tech on duty. I, as CEO, immediately instituted a policy that no one—no exceptions—was allowed to be transferred like that (with jeans on) and everyone had to be only in a hospital gown. That was a decision for the immediate safety of our staff. But it illustrated we needed some more policies to ensure our people and patients are cared for as safely as possible.

We pulled leadership together from different departments and I have tasked them with finding long-term solutions and ideas on safety.

(Note, I have tasked *them*; this goes along with my learning not to be so patriarchal and protective as I once was early in my CEO career.) As it is, the ED is our busiest, and those who work there are already under a lot of stress. Now we were, perhaps, asking them to do one more thing as far as ensuring patients were transported in only gowns. As of this writing, we still do not have our full policy. There has also been some healthy debate, and at times, it can be intense.

But, and here's the big caveat—it is so ingrained in our culture to honor our mission that no one at any of those meetings doubts that everyone else around that table cares deeply about our mission and our people. We may disagree, but we are absolutely of like mind on our purpose.

When you build a culture based on Supercharged Communications, you are also building a place of trust. When you have trust in your leadership and your teammates, disagreements come from a place of "how can we all do this better," not accusations or resentments.

In terms of supporting team members, I will get questions on how to move the needle on KPIs—what do you do when you are not getting the results you want. An example I will use is a department director and the KPI of patient engagement that we have set a goal of 3.5 (out of 5 on a Likert scale). However, the director, for a couple of quarters, has seen that number at 2.5.

The wrong way to go about it is the kind of "scare tactic" speech: "It's been four quarters in a row that you've been below. If you can't get this done, we're going to find somebody who can." The whole threatening methodology does not ever get the best results from people. Employees who do not feel supported do not deliver their best work and best selves.

> **Support and healthy debate do not preclude the tough calls.**

The Appreciative Inquiry approach is (and this was an approach one of our VPs use in real life): "If on this Likert scale of one to five, we were talking about patient engagement, if we were sitting here a year from now, what kind of things happened to get the five? Describe in vivid detail the changes that were made that contributed to a score of five one year from now."

The VP continued: "What are the things that we have to do to make it a five, not a 3.5, not to get from 2.5 to 3.5, but what would we have to do for our patients to give us a five? You know nobody wants to have a party about average. We want to get to *great*."

Support and healthy debate do not preclude the tough calls. Recently, for example, we had some layoffs of support staff and someone at an executive team meeting requested adding a position to his team. Years ago, I would have wasted a lot of executive time with discussion and debate, and I would have kicked the issue or the "hard no" down the line a little. Instead, I listen, but I am truthful. "I appreciate that would be a nice addition to your team, but given our financial situation at this moment, that is not on the table . . . right now."

Sometimes it's a no. Sometimes it's a no for now.

But it will always come down to what is in the best interest for the organization and what our patients need. Our leaders always come back to mission, which I love, and which I think is really effective. We always try to start with what we can agree on.

 Ensure Team Members Feel Informed and Included

I learned a great deal from our former CEO, a larger-than-life man devoted to the hospital. He knew everyone, and was widely admired, with an outgoing personality. However, he was from the generation of

CEOs and leadership who felt if there were six out of six votes from the executive team on something, his vote carried the weight of *seven* votes.

In fact, leadership styles have evolved. Once upon a time, leadership was usually autocratic. It was a hierarchy, fairly linear, and top down. In the last twenty-five years, we've seen that change. Now, leadership is more people-oriented and collaborative. I may be the CEO, but I am part of a leadership team.

In addition, collaborative leadership tries to get us out of our silos. That's why it can be so inspiring working in a hospital. Unlike selling socks, we have a medical purpose and higher cause that unites us (not that the sock company can't be devoted to and love bringing their socks out into the world!).

We now expect leaders to be inclusive. Instead of barking orders or commands, we *inform* and use our soft skills, like Supercharged Communication, to pull people together into a cohesive team.

I will also add to this in our meeting-obsessed work cultures: I try to keep our people informed, while also respecting their time. Meetings must be efficient. If you don't do that, they likely won't ask for a meeting again (and may try to avoid your meetings when you hold them). In essence, in the hospital, if a doctor meets with me during the day, they are volunteering their time. They're getting paid based on the number of patients they see each day, with insurance and pressures to pack as much as possible into their day. If I ask them for a noon meeting, they're meeting with me in lieu of eating lunch! If we do not have content here, and we have a meeting on the calendar, cancel a meeting. You don't have to be chained to it simply because it's in your electronic calendar.

Item	2022			2021		Δ Score	Δ Precentile Rank
	Score	vs. Nat'l HC Avg	Precentile Rank	Score	Precentile Rank		
My work unit works well together.	4.34	0.15	73	4.19	45	0.15	28
The person I report to treats me with respect.	4.46	0.04	55	4.41	46	0.05	9
The person I report to cares about my job satisfaction.	4.27	0.1	63	4.09	32	0.18	31
Different work units work well together in this organization.	3.7	0.05	41	3.63	27	0.07	14
This organization contributes to the community.	4.5	0.24	81	4.35	58	0.15	23
I am satisfied with the recognition I receive for doing a good job.	3.79	0.06	55	3.62	29	0.17	26
Different levels of this organization communicate effectively with each other.	3.39	0.03	52	3.01	16	0.38	36
This organization coducts business in an ethical manner.	4.03	-0.06	37	3.98	25	0.05	12
I am involved in decisions that affect my work.	3.77	0.11	64	3.68	45	0.09	19
I am satisfied with my benefits.	3.71	0.01	51	3.45	22	0.26	29
This organization provides high-quality care and service.	4.19	-0.01	46	4	16	0.19	30
This organization supports me in balancing my work life and personal life.	4.09	0.25	78	3.78	30	0.31	48
I like the work I do.	4.51	0.07	69	4.43	34	0.08	35
My pay is fair compared to other healthcare employers in this area.	3.53	0.23	71	3.16	28	0.37	43
The environment at this organization makes employees in my work unit want to go above and beyond.	3.66	0.13	63	3.42	29	0.24	34
This organization treats employees with respect.	4.01	0.1	60	3.74	21	0.27	39
The person I report to encourages teamwork.	4.3	0.05	57	4.25	46	0.05	11
I am proud to tell people I work for this organization.	4.18	-0.02	43	4.02	17	0.16	26
I would stay with this organization if offered a similar position elsewhere.	3.88	0.05	57	3.65	18	0.23	39
My job makes good use of my skills and abilities.	4.19	0.1	69	4.02	29	0.17	40
My work unit provides high-quality care and services.	4.46	0.1	68	4.32	36	0.14	32
This organization provides career development opportunities.	3.83	0.15	68	3.6	34	0.23	34
I would recommend this organization to family and friends who need care.	4.11	-0.07	36	3.98	17	0.13	19
I respect the abilities of the person to whom I report.	4.29	-0.02	45	4.28	42	0.01	3
I would like to be working at this organization three years from now.	4.11	0.06	56	3.95	23	0.16	33
The person I report to is a good communicator.	4.05	0.03	53	4.03	48	0.02	5
Senior management's actions support this organization's mission and values.	3.92	0.06	54	3.71	21	0.21	33
I would recommend this organization as a good place to work.	4.06	0.05	53	3.89	23	0.17	30
Overall, I am a satisfied employee.	4.04	0.11	63	3.88	29	0.16	34

Build a Structure to Support Key Leaders

When I was conducting my research, I was naturally excited to share it with my key leaders. We started with me and the members of the KSB C-Suite. The concepts I developed were going to start with me . . . then fan out to them . . . then through other leadership . . . and so on (similar to our organizational goals I mentioned before).

Since I am in the healthcare arena, I look at it a bit like the cardiovascular system. Leadership starts at the heart of what we need to do, and then pumps the principles and actions through the entire corpus of the hospital.

That structural model then led to some amazing changes. (And showed me it was working!)

We conducted an employee engagement survey, but its results reflect on the KPIs and measurements I wanted to explore with this new leadership model. It was one thing for *me* to be excited about Appreciative Inquiry and the principles I developed. It was another to be able to measure it in terms of how our employees perceived our culture.

We used Press-Ganey to measure every aspect we could come up with as far as employee satisfaction. And the results were stunning. For example, the statement, "My unit works well together as a team" shot up from 45 to 73 percent. In every single category, we moved the needle. In some, we *supercharged* that movement.

We knew we were onto something.

Earlier in the book we talked about expressing gratitude. That result was proven, too. "I am satisfied with the recognition I receive for doing a good job," in a single year climbed from 29 to 55 percent! (I feel like I have to add the exclamation point there.)

"Different levels of this organization communicate effectively with each other" went from 16 to 55 percent. This directly reflected the way we wanted a collaborative space, not silos.

One I am especially proud of was the question on whether our employees felt supported in work–life balance, which went from 30 to 78 percent. That tells me our employees know we care about their well-being. The fact that the number moved that high on our KPI *despite* the pressures of the pandemic was unassailable proof that Supercharged Communications work.

Our results were so astounding that our Press-Ganey consultant said they had never seen that kind of change in a single year. As we provided leaders with the structures and methodology to elevate communications, it wasn't just a feeling or a hunch that this was working. These were real results from a survey of our employees.

Here's another example of putting in place support. Again, the top-down type of leadership is a dinosaur. So, when we redid our physician compensation program, we brought in physicians to do it. They built our own program. We had an outside consultant to help guide the process. I was in on all of those meetings, as was one of our VPs. But the physicians were the ones that said, "I like this, I don't like this, that's good enough, this isn't good enough." At the end of the day, I presented the plan to our full medical group and was able to say that these eight physicians developed our new plan.

We went in with the idea that we wanted our compensation to be at or higher than the 60th percentile. We achieved that goal—*without* just presenting a plan in which our people had no voice.

The Executive Is Part of the Community—Get Involved

My days of immersing myself in meetings are long gone. This new way of leadership is so ingrained in me that I don't even think that way anymore. Our employee engagement survey data provided proof that my methods are effective, and they can be for you.

As an executive, I think I also had a bit of Imposter Syndrome. (In my experience, just about everyone has a touch of it.) Maybe a small part of me was less involved years ago because (1) the models of leadership until recent times were very much in that top-down mindset, and (2) I thus felt a pressure, as the executive and visible "face" of the hospital, to always have something brilliant to say.

> **It's not about how the community perceives me at all.**

But I realized along the way, I didn't need to be so concerned about how I present myself and what I have to say. It's not about how the community perceives me at all. *It's about me understanding what they have to say.* I don't have to be thinking about what I'm going to say next.

> *I don't have to be interesting.*
> *I have to be interested.*

That's what involvement is. It's relationship. It's all the building blocks we've been doing in this book. I find that incredibly exciting. So my Appreciative Inquiry techniques along with active listening means *I have to be interested.* Wow! That was eye opening.

I spent many years thinking about leadership—if you are reading this book, my guess is you've read all those books too. And they're terrific. I think every single leadership book I read imparts wisdom— even if it's showing me how I *don't* want to lead.

115

But getting involved means I am a learner too.

When I started out as CEO, we did all the community involvement things we should do—sponsor a baseball team, go into schools and talk about various health issues and lessons, speak to the Rotary Club, shake hands, and kiss babies. I especially like the kissing babies part of the gig. But Appreciative Inquiry showed me that getting involved was a two-way street. By connecting with the stakeholders and people most important to me—both at the hospital and in the community—and being *open* to what they shared, instead of sharing just coming from me to them, imparting wisdom I may or may not have had, I saw the world differently.

I can be the Best Part of Their Day. I can reflect to them my commitment to them and our organization.

Recap . . . and a Look Ahead

In this chapter, we focused on some high-level concepts as we have built upon each of our Supercharged Principles. For this one, Be Mission-Focused and Present United Leadership, we looked into that boardroom and at practical leadership techniques. We discussed the "compass" of our mission—how it makes decision-making, disciplinary actions, salary negotiations . . . every single aspect of your leadership . . . more clear.

The five key parts to this principle are as follows:

1. Keep the focus on your mission and know your audience—be prepared.

2. Vocally support team members and encourage healthy debate.

3. Ensure team members feel informed and included.

4. Build a structure to support key leaders.

5. The Executive is part of the community—get involved.

Next, we're going to explore some new things on the horizon of communications. Namely Artificial Intelligence and Appreciative Inquiry. Are the two "AI's" incompatible? When I first started writing this book, I hadn't planned on this next chapter. However, it is impossible to be in leadership and NOT examine the role of artificial intelligence and tech in how we lead.

*Some people call this artificial intelligence, but
the reality is this technology will enhance us.
So instead of artificial intelligence,
I think we'll augment our intelligence.*

—GINNI ROMETTY

AI AND AI

Using Artificial Intelligence to Improve Our Communications

For many of us, our vision of artificial intelligence (AI) was founded in *2001: A Space Odyssey* with its murderous AI, HAL-9000. Or perhaps it was *Blade Runner* or *Westworld* (none of which have a happy ending). Or maybe Rosey on *The Jetsons*. Today, AI is ubiquitous in our lives. Whether that is talking to AI on a Help Desk, ChatGPT and other AI tools, smart homes, or, as it pertains to our discussion, communication tools that use AI.

How does AI inform, augment, or change our communication challenges? Can AI be used with Appreciative Inquiry?

For the purposes of clarity, when I use "AI" in this chapter, I am referring to Artificial Intelligence because most of us associate that acronym with it. When I refer to Appreciative Inquiry, I will spell it out each time, as I have done throughout the book.

It's Here

First, I am reminded of that scene in *The Poltergeist*, where the little girl says, "They're here." Like it or not, AI is here. As a leader, you cannot afford to avoid its impact on your business. First, in terms of staying abreast of your competition, it's essential to know what's out there as far as applications to your sector. Second, it's *here*. It isn't a question of "humans" versus "machines." The fact is, AI will be providing efficiencies in everything from data analysis to cost-cutting and finances. As a leader, you are no doubt already examining how it can benefit your company—or are already committed to its use in one fashion or the other.

However, when it comes to our topic—Supercharged Communications—there's an extra layer to the discussion. Communications are about connecting with people, reaching our constituents, and being the best part of their day. For that to take place while also using AI will require careful thought.

Know When to Use AI and When You Need a Human Touch

AI can be a communication tool, but it's also used for rote tasks or repeatable tasks that don't need a human, per se. For example, scheduling or order processing, data entry-type input, some customer service roles, and assembly line and manufacturing work, to name just a few. Depending on what social scientist you listen to, some people think all this automation will make our lives easier (the better for us to start flying around with jetpacks and having robot maids cleaning our houses). Or it will be the death knell for jobs—and even humanity itself.

I think the most balanced view is that AI will be a job *disruptor* not destroyer. It will make some jobs go away, and it will add others. It will also enhance some jobs (it may take away some rote parts of jobs)—allowing human employees to operate at the top of their license and do more high-level thinking and tasks. Top of license in healthcare means if a certified nursing assistant (CNA) can do some tasks that nurses might ordinarily have to do, then they should handle that, allowing the nurse to use the "top of license" skills they are trained for.

But when it comes to communications, it is good to know when to use AI and when it is important to ensure human interaction. There are times when, even if it is available to you, AI should not be used and a human touch is needed. For example, when you think of creativity, ChatGPT can data scrape and produce answers to questions you ask, but true creativity is a human trait.

AI also does not have emotional intelligence. It can *mimic* emotional intelligence, but it is actually not emotionally intelligent on its own. To that end, when we need to make a human-to-human connection in our communications, it is important we do not rely solely on AI.

For example, you may recall the case of the Vanderbilt associate dean who, along with two colleagues, utilized ChatGPT to write an email to students addressing a mass shooting at another school and urging students and the school community to take care of one another.[38] When the use of ChatGPT came to light, especially considering the gravity of the topic, the dean stepped back from her duties.

This is one of those cases where I think if you are fully human, you understand why it is so important to use AI appropriately when communicating. I don't think it takes someone with a PhD to discern that tragedies, layoffs, bad news, and deeply personal communications, among others, should not be disseminated by AI, and that the communications should be deeply human and empathetic/sympathetic.

Your Mission Is to Make Connections

Why are we here? As a leader, I take out my Life Tree and remind myself: what is my purpose?

I think, as leaders, while balancing budgets is imperative, and steering companies through crises is but one "fire" we have to put out, in the end, we are trying to connect with our key constituents: board

---

38   Jennifer Korn, "Vanderbilt University apologized for using ChatGPT to write mass shooting e-mail," updated February 22, 2023, accessed June 20, 2023, https://www.cnn.com/2023/02/22/tech/vanderbilt-chatgpt-shooting-email/index.html.

members, physicians, colleagues, community members; whoever is most important to you and your organization. It is important to remember that as you consider how you communicate and how, potentially, you can use AI. Whatever your purpose, your mission is ultimately about making connections—without them, a company and your career are doomed.

Leaders who make connections with their teams are rewarded with better performance and loyalty. Without connections (and building trust), jobs can become transactional, without the kind of passion that inspires people to do their best.

Think Additive Not Replacement

If you ever saw *Invasion of the Body Snatchers*—humans were *replaced.* But in actuality, we need to think of AI in communications as an additive. It's a *tool* in your arsenal. Let's go back to one of our essential Supercharged Engagement Principles of communications:

Engage with intent through various mediums.

Communications principles apply—whether you are communicating with AI or you are communicating with Supercharged Principles and Appreciative Inquiry. AI is a *medium.* It is one tool in your arsenal.

The use of AI should also be *intentional.* You will—all of us will—be using it in communications. It is up to us to use human discernment and act with intent to find its *best* uses.

And Not Or: Tools

I've often emphasized to start your communications with *and*, not *but*. In this chapter, let's replace *and* with *or* when it comes to the new tools.

With the rapidity of changes in AI, apps, SaaS, data privacy laws, and so on, no doubt some references will be outdated before the ink is even dry on the printing of this book. No doubt there is going to be massive proliferation of all sorts of tools. Therefore, I thought I would share something about one of the various tools, or *mediums,* we at the hospital have decided to use. It's an *and,* not an *or.*

We make use of video technology called Cyrano. Cyrano bills itself as "artificial empathy for customer interactions."

First, I want to point out the use of the word "empathy" (as well as the attendant "artificial"). While it can be very tempting to feel like AI knows us so well that it is feeling and emotive, or even sentient (not yet, but who knows!), in fact, all AI can do is *imitate* humans. Again, while it can feel scary to see such big disruptions happening so quickly in real time, remember what makes human beings special—our very humanity. Which is something AI will never have.

For me, this tool enables better efficiencies. Every week I get a list of recordings that I need to do, and those are generally anniversaries for our employees or someone that contributed to our GEM awards and include a weekly video to current and past board members. Cyrano allows me to populate my system with whatever I want as far as communications. If I wanted to put in there that I need to make sure that I send a video to each director at least twice a year, it will keep me on track. It is up to me what I put in there as far as my desired cadences. It still doesn't replace that human interaction of small groups, nor one-on-one meetings, and all the things that go with that. It's an *and*—not an *or*—equation.

I utilize it to be more efficient and productive, and to streamline that aspect of my job. It replaces time that I might have spent in typing a personal message or another system that I might use to remind myself of these communications tasks. By the way, this perfectly illustrates *where* an AI tool can be helpful. AI (generally) does not make "human" mistakes. It can do all sorts of calculations, calendar tracking, reminders, data processing, and, yes, communications, that we can sometimes drop the ball on.

In the case of this particular tool, it helps me to make a personalized video, not a mass-produced one. Numerous video retakes are possible, and it's authentic, transparent, and warm. But look at it like this—it is a partnership. *My video, its delivery.*

One other thing that I have found exciting about this tool is the recipients forward it to their family and friends. People generally like to get a personalized message from their CEO or leadership. I've had nothing but positive reactions to this. I could not have done all that scheduling of videos, the video creation, the tracking, etc., without Cyrano, Yet, this tool is something that really has me build visible morale and connections with my teams.

Some of the amazing AI tools for the workplace include apps that make building slide decks faster and simpler; note-takers (no doubt you or your colleagues may be using something like Fireflies); email composers; text summarizers; spreadsheet creators (those of you who cringe at the thought of Excel might welcome this one); grammar checkers and writing assistants; video generators; text-speech generators; voice generators; AI personal assistants; chatbots on corporate websites; and copywriting AI, to name a few types. More are being introduced to the market all the time—and venture capitalists and private equity money, as well as companies of all sizes, are investing in AI.

I have recently started using a product called Lebra Health. Lebra integrates with our payroll system to populate a database with all employees. The tool reminds me of birthdays, work anniversaries, and acts as a customer relationship manager. Although new in its launch, the early returns are fantastic. As I have said previously, when we had just a couple of hundred employees, the personal connections were easy to track. Now I need a little help—and these AI tools are just the prescription for my communications issues.

Disadvantages and Concerns about AI

As with every introduction and leap forward in technology, not everything is great about AI. (You only need to remember HAL-9000 to know that.) It's important that we recognize where, at least for now, it is not always right or even the tool we should be choosing, and that there are limitations to its use.

1. *Lack of personalization.* You may recall at the beginning of the book when our organization was comprised of 350 employees I made every effort to know all of the employees of our hospital by sight and name. For a while, I knew every single person's name, tried to remember all their kids' names and partners' names, and their interests. As we grew, that became virtually impossible, but it sure doesn't mean I don't try. I find that *personal touch* to be essential. It is something I, as leader, can do—that AI cannot. I cannot emphasize enough that the whole purpose of Supercharged Communications is making stronger connections with the people most important to you. AI—even if it can coordinate my video releases, create my slide deck for me at my next executive board meeting, and take notes for me, cannot make the human-to-human connection that is essential for being the best part of someone's day. As I discussed, I use AI to remind me, create messaging, and streamline my communications, but it cannot replace the *truly* personal.

2. *Resistance.* When introducing new AI tools into the workplace, there is understandable anxiety on the part of the workforce. There are, indeed, some jobs that will be on the so-called chopping block. For instance, we have all seen the proliferation of chatbots in customer service on websites ranging from

retailers to our health insurance companies. Those 'bots have obviously eliminated some human jobs in customer service. Between that uncertainty, as well as the proliferation of panicked news stories on the topic, and general unease with both technology and change for some people, there is under-standable resistance to AI in many sectors. Thus, leadership needs to ensure that Supercharged Communications are a part of any introduction to new technology to ensure that as many of your employees' fears are allayed and questions answered.

3. *Potential for communication misunderstandings.* Without the human touch that understands the *nuances* of commu-nications, if you over-rely on AI, you may find some gaps in communications or other forms of misunderstandings. Think of it like this: have you ever found an error in your online banking statement? All of us have, right? But think about what *kind* of mistake. Perhaps a retailer double-charged you for something, or a charge was run through on your debit that was inaccurate. Maybe you canceled a membership for something, and the charge still came out. Or maybe even fraud. However, what I bet you have *not* found is a math error. Depending on your age, if you used to keep your checkbook straight in a checkbook register (PAPER!?), if you found an error in your checkbook, you probably forgot to carry the one. You made a common human mathematical error. With AI, you are going to have accuracy of your figures and numbers. Any errors as far as that is concerned will probably originate with a human being introducing an error into an Excel sheet, etc. On the other hand, we have also all received very awkward or confusing written communication generated by a 'bot at some time. The communication gaps go both ways. Recently, a

friend had to respond to a 'bot-conducted survey in the health-care field. The way the survey was constructed did not allow for any *nuance* about her experiences. Too much black and white and not enough gray. In addition, people (not all) can read nuance on another person's face. For example, someone might say something attempting to be cheerful, but their eyes may be teary, and we know they are faking it. AI is not yet widely able to read those unspoken cues.

4. *Lack of the human touch/REAL empathy.* As someone in the healthcare field, the human touch and empathy is literally the lifeblood of our community. Its "The People." We're all about the human touch. However, I will give you an example of a computer-generated response in the corporate world that demonstrates when tech gets out of balance. I know a woman whose mother passed away. In the chaos and grief of that loss, the woman made a car payment on her mother's car loan, assuming in a month or two, she would sort it out. However, she woke up at 3:00 a.m. in the morning not even thirty days after the funeral to her mother's car being repo'd in her driveway. To make a long story short, the bank (one of the biggest in the United States and one you might recall received negative press about its auto loan division) generated all sorts of actions once they received notification that the loan holder had died, even though it had happened just three weeks before this incident. No human examined this—it was all systems. Communications did not begin with "We are so sorry for your loss" but "We're taking this car because the loan holder is dead" (put a little more professionally than that). AI communication is only as good as the people behind it. Empathy and the human touch need to be built into all

automated communications and AI. I know our hospital will *never* be a place where painful news that needs human delivery is done by a chatbot.

5. *Data privacy concerns.* As part of the healthcare field, privacy has been part of our challenges for a long time now. We all know about the Health Insurance Portability and Account-ability Act (HIPAA), which was passed way back in 1996. But today privacy is an increasing concern across every single vertical because of *data privacy* concerns. AI frightens people because of everything from the risk of hacking of files, to the sheer volume of data it collects. In Europe, the General Data Protection Regulation (GDPR) establishes privacy protections of personal data. Here in the United States, privacy and Big Data stories are daily in the media. The state of California went too far as to pass the California Consumer Privacy Act (CCPA) that addresses some of the same issues. When it comes to communications via AI, we recognize the need for privacy—both for your own sake and the recipient's sake.

6. *Biased algorithms.* AI uses algorithms. If those are flawed, so is the AI. Who is writing the algorithms for the AI? What are their biases? And then how does AI replicate that? An example would be that if you ask AI to give you pictures of CEOs, the AI might present you mostly with pictures of mid-dle-aged to older white males. Since the figures are changing all the time, suffice it to say the number of actual CEOs in the boardrooms of Fortune 1000 companies are white males, and there are not enough women and people of color in leader-ship. As humans, we know that diversity and inclusion are important. But AI produces answers based on data and can

introduce these same biases. There have been biases through-out history, and so data will be skewed in that way. Biases can occur in facial recognition AI (which is more accurate on white faces than faces of people of color), for example. Other biases can be more nuanced. We need to ensure as we integrate AI into our communications, we watch for bias.

7. *Lack of creativity.* Many of us have been playing with ChatGPT or other open-source AI chatbots. Maybe you have seen AI art, generating magnificent digital creations. IBM says that creative AI is our next "moonshot."[39] However, AI cannot create the mystery of the Mona Lisa's smile.

Advantages of AI in Communications

Now let's examine the ways in which AI can be a positive disruptor in our communications.

Customized communications. As I shared earlier, I can make customized videos for people in my hospital. I can send myself reminders for various communications I want to disseminate, whether that's weekly, monthly, or yearly. For people in sales who have been using CRM tools and tech stacks already, this is not news. What *is* news is the way machine learning algorithms can analyze the needs and wants of the people you communicate with and to tailor your responses accordingly. Lebra Health, the CRM product spoken of earlier, used notes entered by me to build communication with the use of AI. This personalization connects your workforce even more, and it helps build relationships—we all want to be "seen," not seen as just a number. We want communications to give a feeling of intimacy and connection. With external communications, this

---

39   IBM, "The quest for AI creativity," accessed June 29, 2023, https://www.ibm.com/watson/advantage-reports/future-of-artificial-intelligence/ai-creativity.html.

helps to improve relationships with your customers and stakeholders. With internal communications, your workforce will be more engaged, and engaged teams at work perform better.

AI can be "taught" empathy. While it's imperfect, as of yet, the new machine learning and AI tools out there are capable of being tweaked (by humans, through programming) to mimic empathy and to be more emotionally responsive. As I said earlier, I don't think I will ever reach a point where I think negative news or (in a hospital setting) traumatic news can be delivered by AI. But AI is evolving by the minute, and there are ways to use AI for efficiencies *and* enhance its communications.

Content creation. We're all looking to streamline our work obligations. Most of us have our top-of-mind tasks that are our priorities. If we can off-load to AI some things that don't require our highest-level abilities, or that will free us up for other work, then we have more time to work at the top of our license and for our *human* interactions.

Measurement and analysis. You may recall that when I undertook this Supercharged Communications journey, I wanted to not just do it but measure it. We have an employee engagement survey—and found that we improved in (to use our survey company's word) "unprecedented" ways. Wow! One advantage of AI is that it can look at our communications efforts and responses and do a micro-examination in ways that help up improve even more.

PR, influencers, and branding. In my rural hospital, we are unlikely to snag some Hollywood star, sports star, or influencer to represent our "brand." But, ever mindful that this book is not just for those in the healthcare sector, I would be remiss if I didn't add that AI is increasingly used for a variety of PR communications strategies. This includes everything from identifying influencers, press release drafts, monitoring social media channels for mention of your brand, and more.

Increased efficiencies. If AI can answer run-of-the-mill basic questions and communications with your company, especially online, this leaves your employees to handle more complex issues—a much better use of their (human) time. Back to that "top of license" thing!

Human errors are largely eliminated. Remember my checkbook and banking example? AI can eliminate some human error—especially if your communications and CRM involve a lot of data.

AI in Healthcare

As the CEO of a hospital, I wanted to take one section to discuss AI as it pertains to my sector.

First, as I mentioned, I have already integrated AI to streamline my corporate communications—especially my internal communications with people on the KSB team, and in particular on an individual basis (which is where AI can shine because of the ease of customization).

I have also used AI to *improve* communications. The program I am using can offer suggestions—I think of it a bit like having someone at my disposal 24/7 to offer feedback and to brainstorm with—in *seconds.* I am sure many of you have, for example, plugged something into ChatGPT, only to watch the answers scroll rapidly down your screen practically before you have finished typing.

One example I wanted to give from healthcare that is an area of promise for AI is its use as healthcare scribes. Those are the people who sit in with you and your doctor and take notes on a laptop, and are often the ones (depending on the practice) who sit with you in the exam room when you first get in there and ask you a series of questions about your symptoms, etc.

This is an important aspect of care because the scribe frees the doctor up. In the "olden days," the doctor would ask all those healthcare and symptom questions, write notes, and those would be transcribed later, etc. Scribes today allow that doctor to come in and get right into the conversation with the patient, already informed.

However, I am sure there is not a single reader who has not gone to the doctor and discovered that someone, whether the doctor, the scribe, a nurse, a tech—a human, got some little (or big) detail incorrect. A friend of mine said it took her three visits before medications she was no longer taking were removed from her "current medications" list. Another person I know told her scribe that she was having significant muscle pain, only to read her own records later when she went to a specialist that said "patient reports no adverse muscle pain."

This is not to "beat up" on scribes. Or complain about human errors in communications. The fact is, it happens, and so my job in communications is *not only* to be the best part of someone's day, but to do everything in my power to serve and protect and honor KSB's patients. There are predictions that AI scribes will take over—thus eliminating potential human errors by scribing what is said EXACTLY.

Before I move on, I wanted to say that I recognize that AI is already replacing scribes, as just discussed, in some practices and hospitals. An important "but" is that we must remember that, by some estimates, 40 percent of the jobs of today did not exist fifty years ago, and 40 percent of the jobs of the future have not been invented yet. Reskilling and upskilling will be essential to keeping our workforce, regardless of industry, current and employable.

Finally, I just wanted to mention that AI in healthcare has incredible potential. AI is better than a human, for example, in predictive analysis—in other words, in predicting disease across a population . . . and in individuals. AI has outperformed radiologists in spotting tumors, for example.[40]

---

40   Thomas Davenport, "The Potential for Artificial Intelligence in Healthcare," *Future Healthcare Journal* 6, no. 2 (June 6, 2019): 94–98, accessed July 1, 2023, https://www.ncbi.nlm.nih.gov/pmc/articles/PMC6616181/.

How Does All This Affect Supercharged Communications?

I went into my research wanting to change the world. Or at least my little corner of it and my hospital. In the midst of my research, COVID upended that world—mine and the entire globe's. When we began to emerge from that, something new was upending the world, at least in a philosophical sense. ChatGPT was released (in November 2022), and the discussion about everything from communications to efficiencies to employment and humanity itself got a lot louder.

However, fundamentally, I realized something very important. In our next chapter, I am going to ask you to create your Life Tree. What are the values and concepts and meaningful elements that populate the branches of your tree? I recently updated my tree (I'll discuss this more in the next chapter). While I made some changes, I realized, like my own internal compass as a person and a leader, that the roots of my tree were very much the same regardless of how my tree evolved and sprouted new limbs and leaves.

This is important for you as a leader to consider. At the end of the day, when we think of our values as organizations, when it comes to internal communications, the preferred order is: people, business, and then finance.

If you jumble that order, it's like a virus in your organization. If you lead with numbers, then you *will* lose people along the way. People are at the core of every business. And that's where it has to do with Supercharged Communications.

AI, data, finances, all of that is part of organizations today. But without Supercharged Communications, those concerns can crowd out your bigger purpose—those things on the tree.

At the end of the day, AI is a tool. But it's just one tool in our arsenal. It's one of those prongs of our communications strategy, but it's not the whole strategy—or even the biggest part. The biggest part starts with *you*.

Our next chapter will discuss initiating Supercharged Communications. And though Appreciative Inquiry and all our techniques start with you, we can never forget the other part of the equation: "The best part of *their* day." Being the best part of someone's day will never start with AI.

Recap ... and What's Next

With the world changing at such a dizzying pace, I cannot possibly predict all the ways in which AI will change the world at large and healthcare in particular. I leave those sorts of predictions to the men and women at the forefront of technology—the big brains.

But this is what I do know. First, as we explored, AI is an "and" tool, not an "or" one. With the right apps, tools, and approach, it can *enhance* your communications, streamline them, create efficiencies, and enable personalization with a few keystrokes. But you as *human* must still put the thought into your approach.

Second, there will always be aspects of communications that require the emotional intelligence of a human. This must be kept top of mind as you choose your tools.

We discussed disadvantages and concerns about AI—from it stifling creativity to bias. Advantages include elimination of some human errors to predictive analysis, and an ability to analyze huge amounts of data to improve the experiences of your constituents.

Next, we're going to look at how to put this all together. Where to start? What to do first?

8

Don't judge each day by the harvest you
reap, but by the seeds that you plant.

—ROBERT LOUIS STEVENSON

PUTTING IT ALL TOGETHER

| *Where to Begin* |

While I will discuss more about my own journey in the final chapter, I want to assure you that at the nascent beginnings of my journey into studying and implementing Supercharged Communications I wondered, "Where the heck do I start with this?" My first excited instinct was to run around trying a little bit of everything. However, you may remember earlier in the book, I was very intentional about not coming back from my weekends at the university so energized over what I'd discovered that I was ready to start first thing Monday and by "start" I mean for everyone.

That simply wasn't going to happen. I took my own measured but no less excited approach.

So, in this chapter, I wanted to offer what insights I can on how to begin and how to apply our Supercharged Communications principles, as well as Appreciative Inquiry, in your organization and life.

Let's start at the very beginning.

Begin with the Tree

When I created my Life Tree, it was very thought-provoking and meaningful to me. First of all, very few of us, in our very busy techedout lives, take the time to sit down and really *contemplate* these parts of our lives. We're so busy making a living that we forget to live, we may forget what our purpose is—if we even knew it to begin with. In fact, I realize what a privilege it was to have this opportunity and to have the kind of educational experience I did. I had encouragement and guidance to examine my values in the context of leadership. Doctoral homework does help one to focus!

The tree helped me crystalize what I wanted for myself—as well as my family, my organization, my bigger community, and even the world.

So, if you are excited about Supercharged Communications, I would urge you to stay excited—but also take this time to create the picture of your values and life and what is truly important to you. I've provided a blank Life Tree for you to fill out (see Figure 8.1).

Take your time. This is something that will inform much of your approach and decisions going forward. Do a rough draft, then fine-tune it after being away from it for a day or two. Allow yourself to think "big" and to be unafraid of aspirational ideas.

The beauty of this tree is that it looks at you as *person* and not just as *leader*. I know as well as anyone that sometimes it can be really easy for the leader side to take over and dominate. That's when we can lose sight of the values we wanted to instill in our lives and our workplaces in the first place. This exercise can remind us that we are not our job.

Remember: Trees Are Living and Breathing

My next piece of advice is super important—so much that I gave it its own section even though it is still about the Life Tree. It is important enough for me to set this off.

Trees are living, breathing organisms.

My Definition of Values-Driven Leadership
One who has an unquenchable thirst for continual learning, challenges existing practices, produces positive results, Innovates to improve the lives of others, and loves unconditionally

Leader as Visionary & Strategist
Continuously scan the environment to identify opportunities to improve the lives of others through innovation and with creativity. Be willing to challenge existing paradigms. Create long-term positive impact.

Leader as Results Driver
Drive clarity around key performance metrics and grow leaders by holding myself and others accountable. Be tough-minded on standards and tender-hearted with people. Embrace the power of **AND** and reject the tyranny of **OR**. We can *always* do better

Leader as Authentic Self
Understand and love myself first. When making change, start small. Be me regardless of the setting. Stay curious and open to challenging my current beliefs. Improve every day. *Wherever I go, I am there*

Leader as Relationship Builder
Make time spent with me the best part of other people's day. Be present, be kind, possess genuine interest and concern for others.

Leader as Teacher and Learner
Strive to be *interested* and not *interesting*. Believe in people more than they believe in themselves. Be curious and challenge theories and beliefs to promote learning. Every piece of granite has a masterpiece waiting to be released.

My Leadership Life Perspective
Improve myself, my family, my friends, my community and the world by writing and speaking about love. Be a missionary for outstanding health, vibrant communities, and spreading love through generosity and healing.

Figure 8.1 The Life Tree of values-based leadership.
Adapted with kind permission from Dr. Gus (James) Gustafson.

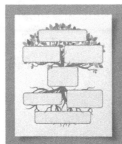

To download your own blank copy, please visit:
www.drdavidschreiner.com

I know, sounds like the writing of this book got to me—but yes, remember that trees are living things. It's important to really think about that because your tree is too.

When I was studying for my dissertation, I can recall the excitement in the room when we were asked to create our tree. We were also instructed to take it out from time to time and work on it—make sure it still represented us and our values. After all, there is the old Heraclitus saying, "No man ever steps in the same river twice, for it's not the same river and he's not the same man."

Our trees will change as we evolve in our leadership.

Out of a class of twenty-four PhD students, only a very small handful of us follow that advice. For me, I do it when I am my own captive audience—for instance, on a plane with few distractions other than my snoring seatmate.

This is an important piece. Please don't skip it. Put a reminder in your electronic calendar to do it at least twice a year, quarterly even better. Not only do we learn more and aspire to do more, but sometimes we achieve some mastery in an area and we decide to pursue a new leadership goal.

Analyze Where You Are Personally

As I said earlier in the chapter, I am grateful I have the time to look at these engagement and communications principles, and so I honor that time by being intentional and focused. Your engagement and communications analysis should be two-pronged: one is a look at leadership and the personal, and the other is an organizational look. Let's revisit our Supercharged Principles—and the approaches beneath them that bring them to life.

Engage & Connect
at a personal level

Engage with Intent
through various mediums

Be Mission Focused
through united leadership

Ask great questions and generate positivity	Find a rhythm of regular communication with key constituents.	Keep the focus on your mission and know your audience—be prepared.
Develop outstanding listening skills and practice them regularly	Be transparent with high frequency.	Vocally support team members and encourage healthy debate.
Be accessible and show an Interest in member concerns	Use multiple channels to communicate your message.	Ensure team members feel informed and included.
Find ways to express gratitude	Look for ways to overcome engagement challenges.	Build a structure to support key leaders.
Find ways to interact through rounding	In times of crisis be intentional about communicating differently.	The Executive is part of the community— get involved.

Look at each one in turn—and I suggest rating where you are right now on a 1–10 scale. Be brutally honest. For this round, rate that on how *you* are doing on each of those fifteen items.

If you are someone who works with a career coach, has an accountability partner, or simply has trusted colleagues or friends or partners you like to bounce ideas off of, you might show them this list and your self-analysis and ask them if they agree with your scores. If their opinion is way off from yours, step back and examine why they might feel that way. If they largely agree, congratulate yourself on your self-honesty and clarity.

Analyze Where Your Organization Is

Next, take all of those criteria and assign a score for your organization. Do you feel the people of your organization embrace these ideals? Do they even know about them—are you modeling them yet? It will be good to see your personal assessment of baseline (though we will discuss professional surveys in a moment). Again, this is a time for radical honesty.

Take a look at both sets of scores on an item-by-item basis. Is there alignment? Sometimes it can be a stunning discovery to see that something you have not valued highly or focused on has a score of 1 for you, and the same could be said of your organization. Consider where there is misalignment and consider potential reasons for that.

Build on Your Strengths

Look at your strengths—and consider how to build on them. For example, if you are already great at being engaged and asking good questions—you're well on your way in Supercharged Communications. But if you have lost sight of your mission and purpose, or if you hide in your office and don't have much employee contact, you need to figure out how to bridge that. If you start with strengths, such as if you are a leader who truly connects at one-on-one meetings—go do more of them. If you are fantastic at giving kudos and expressing authentic gratitude to the people in your organization, think what more you can do to raise the bar.

In terms of your organization, it's been a while (all the way back to chapter 1) but recall our discussion on "Life-Giving Forces." Those are elements of an organization when your organization *shines,* when you are at your most exceptional.

You can use the principles of Appreciative Inquiry in your search and discovery for your strengths. Questions you can utilize:

1. When are we at our best as an organization?

2. What are the stories that show that? Share the details and tell us more!

3. What are the elements in place in those stories?

4. When we're operating on all cylinders, what do you notice?

"I Still Don't Know Where to Start"

I will be honest, I would sometimes lose sleep because I was that excited about things I wanted to try when I began. But as my research developed and I saw *fifteen* areas I needed to address, I felt a little overwhelmed—though I promise it was in a good way.

Still, it reminds me a bit of when people decide to change and have a healthier lifestyle. There's daily walking, drinking lots of water, eating leafy greens, watching calories, getting fresh air each day, meditating, acupuncture, eight hours of sleep a night (if you know anyone who gets that much, let me know), and yoga. If you try to do that all at once, chances are you will be back to your old habits by the weekend.

Here are a few tips on beginning with this methodology:

Seek out themes. You can't customize all of these steps for a thousand different people. Let's look at a communications example. Person A may prefer text messages because she is just too busy to check her emails. Person B may want to hear from his supervisor via a Slack message because they are so immediate. Someone else might want to watch vlogs with a little humor thrown in for good measure. There are as many different communications choices as there are people. In addition, there are differences across cultures (e.g., Orthodox Jews would not welcome a message via technology on Shabbos), across generations (younger people tend to prefer text over emails), and across professions (a police force whose challenges change daily are going to need different message methods than an accounting firm). So, you must seek out themes and trends.

If you have enough people telling you something and there's a theme there or a trend in what you're hearing—it's time to listen. I thought everyone *loved* a weekly message from the CEO. I wanted to be the best part of everyone's week! But instead, the feedback was that was too much—a once-a-month email would suffice.

Ouch.

Actually . . . *not* an ouch. If you are on this journey, it's best to do it without preconceived notions of what "good" communication is—good communication is only as good as how it is perceived and received.

Tell stories when doing it right. When you get started, it's important to tell people when they are doing it right. There may be some growing pains. That's OK. If it was easy, then everybody would be doing it (actually, it would be *fantastic* if everyone *did* do it).

However, you have to tell stories about when it's being done correctly. Celebrate the successes. Celebrate the WOW moments. Celebrate positive feedback from clients and patients and stakeholders. When you celebrate, you promote the continuation of this approach. People decide they want to be a part of this.

In my hospital, I love to talk about our GEM (Going the Extra Mile). I want to talk about those people that serve our community and do that extra bit, even though it's not part of their job. That's why we start every meeting with a patient story because people see that these traits and principles are recognized as positive and important to us all as an organization—and hopefully we all want to do more of that.

Since the cavepeople drew on the cave walls of Lascaux, we have been a society of storytellers. Stories bind us. Stories make the points we are trying to convey memorable. Stories that are emotional imprint on our hearts.

Don't try to change things all at once. It would just be overwhelming. What I did with the five people on our executive team is literally having them rank each of those fifteen actionable steps on a scale of "this sounds horrible and worse than eating lima beans," to "I'm not interested at all" to "when can I start?"

After I got those rankings, I started with the "when can I start" people. Those are your messengers; they are your street preachers, so to speak.

Pick what to try based on what you are interested in. A good rule of thumb is to start with some of these suggestions where you personally might see quick results, or areas you are excited about exploring. If this is something you treat like a child having to eat lima beans you won't succeed. Choose the categories that you are passionate about. When you see results there (and you will!), it will be easier to muster up the energy to tackle the ones you dread a little. For example,

I know an inspirational leader who has a very difficult time with small talk. Even though he *really* cares, he just has a hard time with those sometimes-awkward social interactions. He saved that challenge until he felt confident with some of the others.

Choose your starters. Look at your personal scores from the beginning of this chapter—your personal strengths. For now, cross out anything you got a seven or above. For now, you're good (hopefully one day you'll rank them all up around nine of ten).

Now look at the Bad News Bears section. Pick one that's middling and one that's low. Concentrate on them for the next month. Ignore the noise of things outside of these two principles. Apply yourself, think about it, walk through your organization with intention.

Start with you and fan out from there—next to your C-Suite, leadership, and so on. I started with my leadership. Next, I went to managers. Then, I invited anyone across all departments who might be interested to take a course with me. It's become a "thing." It's the cool kids lunch table.

Measure It

As I have said, we utilized a survey on employee engagement from one of the most respected satisfaction survey companies in the world. One of the more important questions I felt it asked was, essentially, would you tell your friends and loved ones to apply for a job at our hospital. To me that's telling. Maybe you "kind of" like your job. But we don't want kind of. We want ambassadors for KSB, and we want to *earn* that. We watched our scores on that question skyrocket when we started implementing these Supercharged Communications principles. We also measure the success of this through retention.

However, another reason I tell you to measure these concepts is that very often "soft skills" are underestimated. Maybe it's too amorphous for some people. I get it. Which was why, frankly, my fifteen action steps are so clearly written and focused. It's not amorphous. This is all actionable.

And the proof is in the data.

Changing the Culture

We hear the term organizational or corporate culture often these days. While that is usually speaking about the broad overarching culture of a company, obviously one of the most essential pieces of that is corporate communications, both internal and external.

Inc. magazine defines corporate culture as follows:

"Corporate culture refers to the shared values, attitudes, standards, and beliefs that characterize members of an organization and define its nature. Corporate culture is rooted in an organization's goals, strategies, structure, and approaches to labor, customers, investors, and the greater community."[41]

When you decide to "supercharge" communications, don't be surprised if there is a little friction here and there. We ran into our own roadblocks when we instituted this at KSB. There will—in every organization—be those who say, "But we've always done it this way."

Famously, Hubert Joly, former CEO of Best Buy, was of the belief you could change culture much more rapidly than people commonly think. (He actually said in as little as a week!) Usually, people consider corporate change occurring over quite a few years through attrition, retirements, new leadership, new hires, etc. Joly was of the belief that if you change your behavior and you start rewarding the things daily that are consistent with your revised and improved culture, then these modest changes accumulate and they stack on top of each other quickly—and can create big change fast.

---

41   Inc., "Corporate culture," accessed July 1, 2023, https://www.inc.com/encyclopedia/corporate-culture.html.

Supercharged Communications can't be just a phrase (or phase, for that matter). Appreciative Inquiry cannot be something you try for a month or two and then revert to your old ways. This is a cultural change in the DNA of your organization that values every single encounter in your organization being as meaningful as possible.

Spread the Good News

As I've said, you have to start with you. If you are not willing to live these principles, you can't expect your teams to either.

Next, spend your effort where you're going to get a return. I didn't bring the people that were hardest to reach into this process at first. You change culture faster by getting people who are already drinking your positive Kool-Aid. Positive builds on positive. I spread the good news with the people where I was singing to the choir, because I knew they would radiate my message in a way that made a difference.

Win the Middle

This is a concept that has helped me through complications in the hospital's employee relationships. We have over forty departments—all sorts of people and jobs. At the hospital, for example, there are some physicians who are my "fans" (mutual admiration society), and we tend to work well together. There are others who do not love me and they're never going to. I've been at KSB for thirty-five years. Everyone is most definitely not going to be a fan. That's a fact of leadership—no matter how hard we try. That's business. I accept it. I don't take it personally.

But I know to win the middle. I try to craft policies that win that middle and create plans and approaches that the middle appreciates. Your fans are going to like you as long as you don't betray their trust.

The ones who don't like you . . . you may eventually win over! But for now, they are not going to help you enact change.

So you must appeal to the middle, and bring them aboard by demonstrating that your approach is one that will make a difference in people's lives and experiences in and with your organization.

Reviews with Appreciative Inquiry at Their Heart

This approach will change everything about your organization. As you institute it, consider changing the way your reviews are conducted. I fully believe that reviews done from an appreciative approach are far more productive—and better yet, motivating—than the typical approach. That doesn't mean you don't talk about areas for opportunity. Remember one of my mantras is "tough on standards but tender-hearted with people."

Here are some suggestions for how to reframe those reviews into a more supercharged approach using Appreciative Inquiry:

1. Appreciative Inquiry looks to express the ideal—and to use pictures and specific and rich word descriptions to do so. The idea is to make it *real*. Use details and make any aspirational goals as clear and detailed as possible.

2. I always suggest that for people in the first hour of the first day on this new job, you ask, "If you were sitting with your manager a year from now and you talked about the three things that you just knocked out of the park in this, your first year, what are they?"

3. If it is a review where someone is middling, we look to lift them to the next level. In that case, we might say, "If you're at a seven in this area, how would we get from a seven to a ten? And what

impact would that have on the people that you serve, whether that's patients or internal audience or whatever it might be. What will it look like if we make that next step up?"

4. If it's a leader or manager or supervisor who is supposed to hit certain KPIs, we look for the aspirational. "We want to have the highest standards because I know how amazing we are, and we want to provide services that are memorable and that are WOW moments for our patients and their families. No one throws a party for hitting the fiftieth percentile. If next year we moved that up to the eightieth and threw you a parade, tell me what that looks like, what tools you are using, what changes you have instituted?"

Whatever the goals, a culture of fear or shaming produces absolutely no results.

Make Your Values Clear

Many a company has a fancy mission statement. On Enron's website, they touted: "Respect, Integrity, Communication and Excellence." Their four values.

So much for that.

It is important in Supercharged Communications that values are clearly explained and *supported.*

The following statement is true at KSB—and every single, solitary employee knows this. *You will never be criticized for doing something in the best interest of the patient.* According to Johns Hopkins, medical error is now the *third-leading cause of death* in the United States.[42] The

---

42   Johns Hopkins Medicine, "Study suggests medical errors now third-leading cause of Death in the U.S.," May 3, 2016, accessed June 16, 2023, https://www.hopkinsmedicine.org/news/media/releases/study_suggests_medical_errors_now_third_leading_cause_of_death_in_the_us.

number of patient deaths that amounts to is over a *quarter of a million people per year.* Even one is too much.

Our values are very clear. Speak up. It's OK to challenge authority if it has to do with a patient. We are a safe space to question things when it comes to patient care.

You have to *live* the values, not just pay lip service to them.

I also will say that when it comes to ethics there is no gray. That should be clear in all that your organization does.

Look at That Tree Again

All right, I am going to ask you to bring out your tree again. Look at it for a minute.

My guess is, if you embrace values-based leadership, the aspirational elements of your tree focus on how you treat people. You value them! And you want them to know that through your leadership style. I am going to tell you something I didn't realize as a baby CEO:

People are the diamonds of your organization.

Supercharged Principles in Action

In the midst of the COVID pandemic, I was having to conduct my research. Since I was focused on the healthcare sector, it was a scary time. However, it was also a privilege to interview other leaders about how they were using some of the lessons they were learning in the trenches of not just healthcare but communications.

A Community Health System—Staring Down a Global Pandemic

One set of interviews I conducted was with a community health system CEO faced with a pandemic crisis: both financial and in terms of personnel. As a rural hospital, it was essential to its community, but there was also a panicked response. The CEO described the feeling in the community as one of fear and avoidance: "If you go to CHS, you're going to get COVID."

Sometimes when we come out the other side of a crisis we can forget how bad it was. The fear regarding healthcare was real, and it was not unfounded.

State governments shut down elective procedures. This impacted the system's bottom line.

This CEO then faced three concurrent crises: a health crisis, a revenue crisis, and a staffing crisis (all hospitals were having issues in that regard—many employees were sick, or had vulnerable family members). There was also no playbook—the COVID pandemic was like nothing the world had faced since the early twentieth century's Spanish Flu epidemic, but for hospitals, COVID was a three-pronged crisis.

The CEO chose to ask for voluntary payroll reductions, trying to curtail layoffs. He also increased his communications. He sent out a weekly video to all staff, and that video provided details about what was going on. He committed to communicating everything he knew (even at times when we hospitals didn't know too much!).

This CEO practiced full transparency, authenticity, and vulnerability during the crisis. The result was that his employees appreciated his appearing before them, being open with them, and being honest about *not* having all the answers. I can assure you that people will pull behind you knowing you are speaking the real truth of the situation much more than if you try to pretend everything is "fine." I have learned (and am learning) that parental regard for "protecting people" is not consistent with my values nor aligned with their interests.

A Health System Finding Reasons to Celebrate

Expressing gratitude. For some leaders, that is one of the most fun and enjoyable elements to Supercharged Communications. One CEO of a health system explained that he loved celebrations: "Every time we receive recognition from an accrediting agency or receive an award, we get together to celebrate the moment and acknowledge people. We're not the richest hospital around and not the most well-known, but when we get awards, that is a moment to celebrate them … and it makes everyone feel pretty good."

In his own family background, mealtime was a time to share, and he extended that at work by having luncheons and other food-sharing opportunities multiple times each month. For so many of us, "breaking bread" together is a bonding time. I tell this story because that particular way of celebrating resonated with this particular CEO. Therefore, when he had celebrations, it felt very authentic. He genuinely loved interacting with his employees in this way—a manner that was personally meaningful.

> **Presencing is not just showing up. It's putting yourself in someone else's shoes and understanding when it is appropriate to do rounds.**

In addition, this particular CEO embraced rounding. The chief nursing officer would coach him through the process when units might be too busy to spend time with them in the rounding process. If the CNO knew the ER was incredibly busy, he would inform the CEO that it was not a good time. Presencing was on full display at this hospital. I will also add that *not* burdening the ER with a CEO visit when the emergency room was all hands on deck is also a way of presencing. Why? Because it showed the CEO was not oblivious, or worse, arrogantly sweeping through expecting red carpet treatment. He was "with them" as far as understanding now was not the time. Presencing is not just showing up. It's putting yourself in someone else's shoes and understanding when it is appropriate to do rounds.

It Doesn't Stop at Work

One of the more exciting elements of Supercharged Communications is that once you start seeing opportunities for this sort of communication, you will apply it across all aspects of your life.

Communications is not just how you send out an email or tweet. It's not just vlogs and media. It's not even rounding and personally meeting with people. At its heart, communications is connection, one person to another. Think of it as two people who speak totally different languages. One person speaks English and the other speaks Mandarin. These languages could not be more different from each other. Unlike, say, French and Italian or German and Austrian having some elements that might invite a little bit of understanding or familiarity, English and Mandarin afford no such help. If these two people cannot find a way through pantomime or a translator on their phones/ tech to "speak" to one another, communications will be nil. There will be no connection.

We need to connect. But not just at work.

While we probably spend one-third of our lives at work, that is not the only place we need to be "presencing." Supercharged Communications and Appreciative Inquiry are also techniques you can use in your personal life, in relationships with friends and families and loved ones—as well as encounters in the community, etc.

I'll give you an example. An acquaintance recently stopped his tween in the midst of a teenage tantrum upset over transportation issues and a soccer tournament. Instead of being solution focused, his daughter was getting more and more upset. The fact that he had been unable to connect with another parent—they were playing phone tag—over carpooling only made it worse. Of course, he was to blame! But this dad paused and asked, "If this problem you are upset about was fixed and everything went the way you wanted, what would that look like and how can I help you?" He looked for solutions instead of feeding into her panic.

You can imagine many partner relationships where these principles apply and would work very well. We often hear, for example, about love languages. Sometimes our partner needs x, and we just keep trying to give them y instead of asking and listening. If your marriage or relationship has reached an unhappy juncture, you could ask, "If a year from now we were the happiest we've ever been together, what would that look like?"

Then listen. Carefully.

You can also see how in conflicts small and large, from disagreements with siblings to parent–teacher conferences, from customer service complaints to difficult conversations with someone in our lives, the situation could be de-escalated by applying these principles.

I picked six elements, and edited them ever-so-slightly, to show you how these ideas can be life-changing, not just in the workplace but in "real life."

Ask great questions and generate positivity.

Develop outstanding listening skills and practice them regularly.

Be accessible and show an interest in your partner or family member's concerns.

Find ways to express gratitude to your loved ones.

In times of crisis in your family be intentional about communicating differently.

Ensure your family members feel informed and included.

However, I will let you in on a secret. These principles eventually become part of your DNA. I cannot imagine *not* asking Appreciative Inquiry questions in conversation now. I cannot imagine working with someone—whether that is in the workplace or manning a bake sale table or coaching Little League—and not expressing sincere gratitude for their help. I cannot imagine hiding from a crisis in my office—or away from my family—instead of being present and transparent.

Recap . . . and a Look Forward

In this chapter, we looked at how you can start applying these principles in your leadership, as well as how to approach bringing more people aboard to spread the DNA of Supercharged Communications. We reviewed *all* the principles.

Engage and Connect at a Personal Level

1. Ask great questions and generate positivity.

2. Develop outstanding listening skills and practice them regularly.

3. Be accessible and show an interest in member concerns.

4. Find ways to express gratitude.

5. Find ways to interact through rounding.

Engage with Intent through Various Mediums

1. Find a rhythm of regular communication with key constituents.

2. Be transparent with high frequency.

3. Use multiple channels to communicate your message.

4. Look for ways to overcome engagement challenges.

5. In times of crisis, be intentional about communicating differently.

Be Mission-Focused and Present United Leadership

1. Keep the focus on your mission and know your audience—be prepared.

2. Vocally support team members and encourage healthy debate.

3. Ensure team members feel informed and included.

4. Build a structure to support key leaders.

5. The Executive is part of the community—get involved.

In addition, we analyzed both where we were personally as well as organizationally. Finally, I truly encourage you to embrace these principles not just at work but in life.

Next, I'll share some thoughts on where my journey started and where it is now—and what it all means.

Culture does not change because we desire to
change it. Culture changes when the organization
is transformed—the culture reflects the realities
of people working together every day.

—FRANCES HESSELBEIN

HOW CAN I HELP?

A New Lifetime of Supercharged Communications

You know those "How it started, how it's going" memes?

Let me tell you how this journey started for me and how it's going right now—this very minute as I am writing this.

My path to Supercharged Communications started four or five years ago with me being confronted in a restaurant about a hospital bill that was not itemized as we'd promised the patient's family. Only that wasn't *really* what it was about. And that wasn't even the real start of it all. It was just a symptom of things that were wrong.

That bill was about how I felt when someone had a problem and I wasn't sure how to fix it—beyond just trying to get it done so the person wouldn't be upset anymore. I spent a lot of time "fixing" things and not enough time on the people part. In addition, part of the "virus" in my hospital was about a lack of transparency in sharing bad news—I just wanted everyone to think I could handle it all. I was a newer CEO, and I had this false belief or construct that I had to have all the answers all the time.

How It Started

My journey started when I realized I was hiding in meetings focused on the hospital's bottom line, instead of being part of the lifeblood of the hospital itself.

It started, to be honest, with a burned-out CEO.

I don't know that, if you had asked me then, whether I would have said I was burned out. I think I tend to equate burnout with the kind of first-responder burnout the healthcare heroes who work in hospitals contend with daily, especially in the age of COVID and what they went through during the ravages of the pandemic. There are professions—police, fire, surgeons, social workers—where burnout is a real threat by the very nature of the job. But the rest of us are not immune. As a CEO of a hospital, within a community I care about, I was a little burned out, too. Maybe more than a little. Or maybe a better way to put it is that I had lost my edge, my fire; I had forgotten why I decided to not only work in a rural community in its rural hospital, but to *stay* there and become its CEO—as a person truly invested in this place and its people in a very real and potentially powerful way.

So that's how it started. Not promisingly. It started with a weariness I had a hard time putting into words.

How It's Going

First, I suppose I should say that to get *here,* to where I am right now, I had to be open to a spark of inspiration when a colleague talked to me about a doctoral program that might be the perfect "cure" for what ailed me. I had to be accepted and then go through a rigorous PhD program. I had to choose my subject matter for research. I had to go back and forth to a campus, on top of my usual responsibilities. I had to adapt to tech. I had to adapt to tech a second time when COVID arose. I had to do a *lot* of research in addition to my "regular" job as CEO. I had to interview many of my colleagues and peers. Then I had to take all that research and assemble it into a set of principles that could be applied—not just in my life and the lives of the people in my hospital and community, but as applied to all people, regardless of sector, who were looking to communicate better. But it was more than even that. It was about more than just learning to engage *better*—it was learning how to help those looking to completely transform how they communicated with the people most important to them.

I think for all our tech, for all our wired lives, for how busy we are and how many people are part of our world, we communicate worse than ever before (proof: don't ever read the comments on any news story—even a story that seems innocuous). I started on my journey seeking to change that, looking for methods to initiate Supercharged Communications. I sought to do communications in a more powerful, positive, and meaningful way.

So, how's it going?

My life has completely changed.

The world has changed, and I was a part of it. We all were. I and the people around me at KSB Hospital had to go through COVID as part of the healthcare industry—and as citizens of the world. We had to confront a health crisis unlike any seen in my lifetime—or even my parents' generation's lifetime. We as a hospital community and a state and a country had to deal with horrific loss. The healthcare industry, and countless hospitals along with ours, had to face a financial earthquake caused by that same public health crisis.

We've been through a lot.

And yet, how's it going?

Surprisingly, it's going in an inspiring way, even though many of the problems remain the same. But I go through each day with an energy I did not expect.

I don't go to bed staring at the ceiling wondering how I'm going to handle the issues of the hospital (as often). I may not have all the answers, but I know

> **I go through each day with an energy I did not expect.**

how I'll communicate the answers I do have and any uncertainty that I am struggling with. I never wake up sighing anymore. Each day is different and an exciting challenge. I don't inwardly cringe if someone approaches me a little upset about something at the hospital. I view every encounter as an opportunity to learn and get better, or to be the best part of someone's day. I'm in a race against myself on how to up my communications game every day. For me, it's fun to come to work and be part of this place because of the way that we engage.

That's how it's going.

The Culture of Supercharged Communications

Supercharged Communications is a methodology of three main principles with real, actionable elements—fifteen of them in total. You could do one or two. You could do five. You could aim for all fifteen (which is what I recommend—but over time). How you and your organization execute these parts to the whole will be as varied as there are people reading this book from across all sorts of sectors, verticals, and experiences. How you apply it in your leadership life—and in your personal life—is only limited by your vision of how Appreciative Inquiry can change your relationships with the people most important to you.

When I set out on this journey, I was interested in *communications*. I think if I had set out to "change the culture of the hospital"—it would have felt much too huge. Not that I thought our hospital had significant problems—we were "OK," doing "fine." But we all always want to improve. However, KSB has over forty departments and many people. Changing the culture? That would have felt a bit presumptuous. A huge undertaking. How?

Yet these Supercharged Communications principles, with people at their core, really do change an organization's culture from the inside out, with intention—and with a bit of osmosis. I can recall, when I was new to this, getting a much better outcome than I expected because of Appreciative Inquiry and secretly thinking, "It worked! It worked!" The next time you have to deal with a complaint of some sort in your role at work, I challenge you this: ask, "If I could fix this in a way that exceeds your wildest expectations, what would that look like? Tell me about it." See if that doesn't shift the energy in the room right away.

We often read that changing culture is a multiyear process, and there are stats and executive leadership books and all sorts of articles that you can read as far as that topic goes. I think the typical range quoted is a minimum of eighteen months, on up to about five years. It just depends on the thought leader whose views you ascribe to and the numbers they quote.

And that's great. Change usually isn't overnight. But as I mentioned earlier, the CEO of Best Buy, Hubert Joly, for example, believes change can be rapid, especially if the CEO and leadership are very intentional and clear from the outset. This can start with emphasizing and rewarding the new desired traits and being very selective with your new hires to ensure they embody your vision. If you were to ask yourself, "What's one thing I can do right now that will make everything else easier," I suggest the answer might be supercharging your communication. It *feels* more doable than changing corporate culture.

Another reason that cultural change can occur more quickly than expected sometimes is that often your employees know the workplace is toxic or has issues—you may, in fact, be the last to know (especially if you inherited, or unwittingly created, a culture of fear). But when, at last, toxic leadership is pushed out, it can have a profound "ding-dong, the witch is dead" excitement around it. Ideas for change can then bubble up quickly.

Changing Myself

I think the hard part for many business leaders is measuring change—including in ourselves. Everyone does not do employee engagement surveys like the healthcare sector tends to. Patient experience and employee engagement are a hospital's essential elements. Engagement surveys are tremendous tools to analyze areas for improvement, as well as homing in on what your employees are passionate about.

I think it's also difficult to gauge personal progress sometimes. An organization can have data at their disposal, but our own progress as human beings can sometimes be a bit vague. Very often, we don't see our progress until we come out on the other side. Think of your own personal growth. For many, if not most of us, growth tends to come from pain, or from circumstances that push us to grow. But as we're going through it, we are in a forest/trees situation—and often can't "see" our growth until we claim the wisdom awaiting us on the other side.

Sometimes, we have a tangible goal—like a fitness goal. We want to achieve lifting this weight for this many repetitions, or we want to be able to run this distance. Personally, I've been on a diet since 2012. We might have a goal to earn a certain degree, which we achieve class by class as we take each course required by the college program. We might have a goal, in healthcare, to obtain a specific licensure. These are measurable achievements. You pass a test or you don't. You lift the weight or you don't. You cross the finish line of the 10K or you don't.

But there is an element of Supercharged Communications that is about how you *feel* internally when you are interacting with the people who are important to you. While we can rank our feelings on a scale of one to five or one to ten, the fact is, they're *feelings*. They are not perfectly measurable in any exact way. All I can tell you is my experience. And my experience is that I see and feel the difference when I deal with people. That's the part that's given me the real energy. I *know* I'm engaging with the people around me at a different level. And that's been beyond fun. (Yes, *fun*.)

We used to think it took only about three weeks to change a habit. So personal transformation gurus would often tell people to replace a bad habit with a new, positive habit for three weeks or so and you were well on your way to personal change. For example, if you were a smoker and instead chewed gum every time you wanted a cigarette, after a while, that new gum habit would feel automatic. If you wanted to eat healthier and analyzed your eating habits and knew that lunch out with your coworkers was a time when you indulged four days a week, for three days each week you could replace lunch out with bringing a healthy lunch and a walk around the nearby park. After a month, this would be a new habit. Who knows, you might invite friends to brown bag it and walk too and find an accountability partner or two along the way.

However, we now know that it can take forty, fifty, sixty days or longer to really change a habit. Even longer than that if this is a very ingrained mindset of many years, or a so-called muscle memory. Have you ever moved, and months later suddenly found yourself taking the old route home because it was still stored in your brain as your go-to? I know someone who switched from a key ignition to a keyless, and nearly a year later, she still fumbles for her "keys."

It is also, according to some, easier to change a physical habit than a mental one. As an example, if you have a bad back and relearn how to sit properly so your back hurts less, it will take a while, but you will learn *that* much more quickly than a mindset you have to pause yourself from going to as your usual thought pattern.

Appreciative Inquiry is very much an optimist's approach. The very act of Appreciative Inquiry is about asking what things would look like—if everything were perfect. If you knocked it out of the park. Appreciative Inquiry suggests aspirational impact. If you are used to your first thought being cynical about everything, it is going to take real effort to change your thinking to this new habit of positivity. It will take a while until that is second nature.

For me, because Supercharged Communications are not a single habit but a whole mindset, I think it took the different elements three to six months to become natural for me and to meld together fully. I remember in those first weeks, my old mindset would kick in almost automatically, and I'd try to catch myself before I said something, and then speak the new thought that I had around asking Appreciative Inquiry questions. It was almost like a mental hiccup—my first instinct . . . and then the self-correction of asking a "great" question.

Eventually, I stopped thinking about what technique I was trying to apply and instead just reacted naturally—in my new thought pattern. I reached the point where I didn't have that first thought anymore—the "old me." I rarely have to catch myself anymore. And I actually give myself a pat on the back, which is not a natural thing for me, when I do catch myself leaping to an appreciative approach. Rewards, even internal ones, encourage desired behaviors. This is part of who I am now. It's fully integrated into my programming. (Or am I AI? Actually—I told my publisher I was going to tell my readers that this entire book was written *without* AI. This is all me!)

I also think it helps to view this in a nonjudgmental way. Do not think of it as "bad" or "good" habits (like the smoking habit versus the gum habit) but instead as the old way and the new and improved way. There's more gray to this than you might think. The old way wasn't necessarily wrong or terrible. It just no longer serves you as well.

You need to learn a new and better way.

Think of it like this: if a baseball player needs to learn a new swing because they are not getting the results they want and their batting average is .163 (if you don't follow baseball, that really stinks), a new batting coach will come in and analyze the old swing. They will watch the player hit in the batting cage and against a warmup pitcher over and over again. The coach will film the player. They will break that film down in slow-mo. Frame by frame. Then the coach will point and say, "There—that way you lean right as the pitcher releases the ball is not getting the best power out of your swing."

First, the player has to realize they are doing that. Even if they see it in the frame on the screen, they will have to "feel" it as the pitch comes at them a few times. Fine, now they recognize it. Next, the player will learn the new approach. But at first, they're going to fail. A lot. Because they probably learned that swing back in Little League. And then maybe their college coach saw nothing wrong with it, so that muscle memory is strong. The new swing is going to feel strange. Wrong. Certainly not fluid. In fact, the player will have to think about it each time. But after thousands and thousands of swings, the new swing will be second nature. The player will suddenly be batting .381. The same applies to the golf swing. Change happens slowly and then quickly.

But . . . the player still has to watch their swing. In times of stress, I think it's very easy to fall back into your old habits. It's easy to return to baseline.

My Baseline

My baseline—my old baseline—was a healthy dose of FOMO along with a tendency to get into the weeds with numbers and meetings and the "business" of my job.

I used to, for instance, worry that if I said no to a meeting of any sort this would be bad for my leadership. My "fear of missing out" would rear its head and I'd think, "If I don't go to this one, they'll never invite me again." I have since learned to resist that return to baseline. Not getting invited again is a risk I choose to take. And, to be honest, that hasn't come to pass. (Which is another life lesson—we can spend a lot of time as leaders spinning our wheels over every potential eventuality—when maybe none of those possible outcomes will come to pass.)

I also know that my other baseline instinct—to go down a rabbit hole of spreadsheets and numbers and meetings and more meetings—does not help me, our leadership team, our hospital, or, most especially, our patients and their families. Supercharged Communications have very little to do with finance. It took me a long time to realize that the best way to get improved financial results is to hire a world-class chief financial officer. That role is one I can't and don't want to fulfill. Hire great people and get out of the way and coach them to success.

The KSB motto isn't far off. It's the people.

I know, too, there are many CEOs (less so over time as we learn this does not produce the best long-term results) whose baseline is to "lose it" over bad news. I promise you that you can't do this kind of communications change in a culture of fear. People cannot embrace Supercharged Communications and start to relax into being less numbers-focused and more people-focused if at the first hiccup, baseline is right back into the place of negativity. That can set back progress months—or even years. It says to your colleagues and team, "This is a lot of talk and not really part of our culture or important to me."

Supercharged Communications need a climate of collegiality. That is the ability to work with colleagues in a supportive environment. That sort of openness and supportiveness is a top-down directive. It must be modeled from the C-Suite and then through every aspect of your organization. Emotional safety or psychological safety in the workplace is a company where employees feel comfortable pushing back, raising concerns, where they feel secure, where they do not fear scorn or public humiliation.

It's the company where the CEO doesn't excoriate everyone at the board meeting. Less psycho, more supportive.

Rather than calling out any particular leader, suffice it to say, we've all heard of the brutal CEOs who expect work commitments at the sacrifice of all other aspects of their employees' lives. (I know someone who worked for one of

Supercharged Communications need a climate of collegiality. That is the ability to work with colleagues in a supportive environment.

the big four accounting firms and at crunch time would sleep under her desk.) We all know or have heard of CEOs who demean their teams and demand results—or else.

That approach cannot work with the principles in this book.

But what do you do if you do backslide to your baseline? And believe me, it will happen. What if you have been trying to communicate in this new and improved way and you blow it? How do you recover from that? Let's say you have the "lose it" moment: do you ignore that you had it? Not if you have committed to better communications.

I'll share a personal story that literally happened last week—a small example of backsliding and recovery, of having a bad moment and fixing it through Supercharged Communications.

Our board of directors was assembling at an off-site meeting about three hours or so away at a hotel. This was extremely important, and we needed our key people there—we had a lot of decisions to make and information to impart. That same week, in addition, our chief of staff was also in charge of an annual big road race that we have here in town. I was expecting our chief to be at the board meeting on Wednesday. The day before the board meeting, on Tuesday, the chief sent me a text that said something came up and it was related to work for her and she might not be able to make it. My first response was very blunt: "If this is about work, you can make it here. This is more important. If it's about the race, then just say so."

Cringe.

As soon as that text left my fingers, I regretted it. That is actually not even my typical baseline. I was just . . . stressed and sent something unhelpful and even a little jerky.

I could have ignored that I sent it. Just pretend I never did. Move on.

That wouldn't be the Supercharged Communications way, however.

Instead, Supercharged Communications really demand that I make things right—we need to be intentional in communicating, and leadership needs to feel supported. My text did not pass either of those two aspirations. So my chief and I just talked about it. When she did come down to the meeting, because we could have the conversation in a culture of honesty, I said, "This was an extremely important meeting for us. This was like our Super Bowl, and this one was off-site, so I had more anxiety about it than I do when we have one in our own boardroom." I offered vulnerability. "I didn't know the technology; everything was different. I needed my A-team here."

I apologized for the way I said it—Supercharged Communications are often not about *what* you say but *how* you say it. "But I really could have worded that so much better. And I'm sorry."

The more honesty we have, the more our teams have the space to be real. But honesty means being frank—not being brutal. Ask yourself before you open your mouth, "Is what I am about to say helpful?"

I had to dare to do something different in my workplace—and in my life. I had to change my baseline. Not just change the way I lead but I needed to learn new tools that allow me to do so while moving forward with empathy.

How Can I Help?

Most of the people I know go into healthcare because they want to help people. I know I did. I also knew I was interested in returning to rural Illinois. I have always found, as I often tell people, something deeply honorable in our small towns, on our farms and within the fabric of our communities, and, in particular, in the people that make up my hospital and my community of Dixon and Lee and Ogle Counties.

I wanted to help. We may think of "helper" professions as those in, for example, healthcare, teaching, or social work. But regardless of your profession, there is the adage in business that you are not selling a product but a solution. You are helping people—whether you are providing a service, leading a rural hospital, or have a B2B product that helps your customers solve a business problem.

I know my purpose is to help people, so I am always looking for the best way I can be of service. The reason that I wrote the book is I went into this whole process saying, how can I find ways to connect with the people that matter the most to me? In the process, I found some—and now, to help you, my readers, I wrote this to share those ideas and techniques—and help even more people.

I love helping other organizations and other people learn to supercharge their communications. At a recent panel I was on about this very topic, I stayed and talked to the many people who wanted to ask me questions after. When you are as excited about a topic as I am about this, it is energizing to be around people who want to talk about it, too! That's because it fits in with my entire mindset, which is: how can I help? Sometimes, I know I am preaching to the choir—people passionate about communications. But having, say, an actionable list of fifteen traits is about more than preaching—it's about doing.

Values Don't Change

At its heart, Supercharged Communications are values-based (remember, our Life Tree is very much about what we value and hold dear). These values do not shift according to circumstances.

You know that scene at the end of *The Wizard of Oz* when Toto pulls back the curtain? It is, of course, the perfect visual metaphor for a person presenting one way—and turning out to be someone different. I think we have all been disheartened in life by being a fan of a person—from ballplayer to musician to simply someone we admired in our lives—only to discover that the public face of the person does not match the private.

Supercharged Communications rely on real principles of integrity, leadership, honesty, and more. These are not values of convenience. They are values that we live—and they don't change in different circumstances. When Toto pulls back the curtain, the same exact person should be back there.

That is another thing I learned in my journey. This is who I am—this book. It is what I believe in. It doesn't change on Monday if we have a bad day in the ER. The fifteen principles are the principles—not when they are convenient or when they are easy to do.

Maybe that is why I review my Life Tree often, as an important part of my life. I don't want to drift too far from who I am. If this sounds a little like a "faith," I suppose it's because it's values-based. In other words, if you want to be a "good" Christian, Jew, Muslim, Buddhist, Hindu, or Wiccan (to name but a handful of the world's religions), it should not be only when you are in your church, temple, or mosque that you behave as a "good" person. Your faith is something that should thread through all the areas of your life. A mentor once told me to lead my life as if every action would be on the front page of *The Wall Street Journal*. My values when it comes to my Life Tree and Supercharged Communications do not change.

Authenticity Doesn't Change, Either

I think when you start down this path toward Supercharged Communications, it's helpful to realize that this is you—only better. In other words, David Schreiner—regular me—tries not to be a jerk. He genuinely likes people. He loves his hospital. He is always looking to improve himself. He is always looking to be helpful. And he does or says a minimum of two stupid things every day. That guy? He's the same guy who does Supercharged Communications—these techniques just help him do all those things and be all those things . . . better.

It's interesting, I have met a lot of leaders who fall into one of two camps. The ones who think going on CNBC or speaking to a thousand people at a conference is fun, but for whom small talk is torture. And the ones who love that one-on-one but dread the big presentation. I actually think for either type of person, Supercharged Communications will help you. Who *you* are is hardwired into you. These methods only take who you are and enhance the level at which you communicate.

A Challenge

As adults we learn by doing. By placing ourselves in situations and intentionally creating change. I want you to pick two things out of the fifteen Supercharged Communications methods that you're going to do this month—and watch what happens as a result. I'd love to hear from you at my website www.drdavidschreiner.com about your experiences. What changes occurred? How did *you* change? What was exciting about the results? How did it alter the way you communicate?

Next, I would invite you to spend the next month typing into your phone, or scribbling into a little journal, anything that touches your heart and soul over the next four weeks as it related to *connecting* with people whether at home or at work—especially as it relates to Supercharged Communications. Write down your experiences. See how those little moments relate to your Life Tree. At the end of these four weeks, update your tree.

What encounter showed you that this methodology is life-changing?

The biggest thing for me is once I began to understand Appreciative Inquiry and the idea of asking great questions and dreaming about how things could be better, that fundamentally changed the way I looked at the world in a very positive way. It just made me want to be "in it" more, whatever it was. Whether it's at home with your grandkids or kids or with your partner, or interacting with all the people you meet at work, it's just exciting to move through your day in a Supercharged way! Thanks for taking this journey with me. I look forward to hearing from some of you!

ACKNOWLEDGMENTS

I am grateful to have been influenced by several individuals who have exemplified leadership through their behaviors, communication, and perseverance. They all shared their ability to motivate me to exceed my limitations.

For many, our first experience with leadership comes from our fathers. I am fortunate to have a father who always encouraged me to explore different perspectives and consider the broader context. My dad instilled in me the values of hard work and effective organization, which have proven to be keys to success.

Many of us learn about leadership from our coaches, often our early mentors. I was fortunate enough to have a track coach in high school named Lyle Hicks, who taught me the importance of positivity. Coach Hicks had a strict policy against using the word "can't" and instead encouraged us to believe in ourselves and strive to exceed our limits. Even now, I reflect on his teachings and apply them to my daily life.

I succeeded a legendary hospital CEO, Darryl Vandervort, who led KSB Hospital for more than twenty-five years. His strategic brilliance and personality were evident daily, and I learned more from him than any classroom experience could offer.

Dr. Joe Welty has been practicing family medicine in our community for many years and is highly regarded. He has been a great friend and a valuable sounding board for me. His approach always emphasizes the significance of faith, family, and friendship in every interaction.

Colleen Henkel is a respected leader in the community, serving as both a local bank president and a two-time chair of KSB Hospital's board of directors. Her actions and presence demonstrate the power of combining class, grace, and intelligence with humor and kindness to achieve success. Mrs. Henkel's leadership continues to be an inspiration to me.

Dr. Jim Ludema has taught me how to practice Appreciative Inquiry. His enthusiasm and zest for life inspire me to lead more positively and strive to be the highlight of someone's day. He is often the highlight of mine.

One of the most rewarding aspects of my career has been the opportunity to work alongside the exceptional men and women who selflessly contribute their time, energy, and talents to the KSB Hospital board of directors. To each and every one of you, thank you for the invaluable lessons you have imparted and continue to impart and your unwavering support toward the hospital and its mission. I feel truly blessed to be a part of such an extraordinary team. Thank you for making a profound difference in my life and in the lives of so many.

Throughout my time at KSB Hospital, I have had the privilege of working alongside numerous leaders within and outside the healthcare industry who share a deep commitment to serving our patients and their families. Your dedication is admirable, and I am grateful for the opportunity to work with you.

Finally, I would like to express my heartfelt thanks to my wife, Stephanie, my children, Andrew and Kaile, and my grandchildren. Allowing me to be a part of our family is a blessing, and I am grateful for it. They bring me immense happiness, and I treasure every moment I spend with them. To all of you, I love you.

ABOUT THE AUTHOR

DR. DAVID L. SCHREINER is a passionate advocate for rural hospitals, having spent most of his life in small towns and working in small communities.

David considers himself a values-driven leader, striving to make progress every day in meeting his definition of values-driven: *One who lives in the moment, has an unquenchable thirst for continual learning, challenges existing practices, produces positive results, innovates to improve the lives of others, and loves unconditionally.*

David's life and leadership perspective is driven by improving himself, his family, friends, community, and the world with optimism and love. He aims to be a missionary for excellent health and vibrant communities, spreading love through generosity and healing.

His research focuses on improving the health of others, with a particular focus on rural communities.

David is a past member of the Board of Governors of The American College of Healthcare Executives. David is the past American Hospital Association Rural Health Task Force chairman. He was the 2007 Dixon, Illinois Citizen of the Year and received the 2022 Distinguished Alumni Award from the University of St. Francis College of Business.

David and his wife, Stephanie, have two children, Kaile Valdez and Andrew Schreiner, and two granddaughters, Klara and Nova Valdez, with a third grandchild on the way.

Printed in the USA
CPSIA information can be obtained
at www.ICGtesting.com
JSHW081227201223
54088JS00001B/1